# WRITTEN BY THE FINGER OF GOD
(Exodus 31:18)

A look at

## THE TEN COMMANDMENTS
(Exodus 20:1-18)

By

Dr. Stanley R. Hendricks

Published by The Hendricks Service

# Copyright ©2004
## Dr. Stanley R. Hendricks

All rights reserved. No part of this book may be reproduced in any form, except for the inclusion of brief quotations in a review without permission in writing from the author or publisher

International Standard Book Number: 1-59196-600-0

Library of Congress Control Number: 2004107196

First printing
June 2004

Additional copies of this book are available by mail
Send $15.95 each (includes postage and handling) to:
The Hendricks Service
P.O. Box 882
Adel, GA 31620
(229) 896-1355
Order on line
www.drstanleyhendricks.com

Printed in the U.S.A by
InstantPublisher.Com

**Dedicated to my wife**

**Mary Laverne Hartley Hendricks**

**She has been a faithful wife, the loving mother of our two children, and a great friend to me.**

**I really don't know how I could have survived without her by my side the past almost fifty-two years!**

**She is second only to God in my life.**

**With all my love and gratitude!**

## ACKNOWLEDGEMENTS

The author is indebted to many persons for their contribution to this work. Some, I am sure, I do not know by name or have not realized that they made a contribution. This may have happened because I have learned so much over the years from so many different teachers and preachers. However, I must list those that I know have contributed directly to this work:

<u>My father</u>: Rev. Sam L. Hendricks, who was such a great preacher, and from whom I learned how to, and how not to do so many things.

<u>Jane Merritt</u>: She is a dear sister in the Lord who has been such a blessing to my wife and me. She gave me my first computer so that I would have the means to put my thoughts in written form.

<u>Dr. James Griffith</u>: Former Executive Director of the Georgia Baptist Convention, a great friend and boss before, during, and after my thirteen year tenure with the GBC.

<u>Ellen Alderman</u>: Former English teacher. While I was her pastor she took the time to read the manuscript making sure the grammar is correct, and other valuable suggestions.

All Scripture passages quoted are the author's modification (MKJV) of the original King James Version of the Bible: comparing the Hebrew, Greek, and other modern translations to arrive at the clearest meaning possible, and yet stay as close to the King James Version as possible.

<u>Terri Webb</u>: Christian Artist Extraordinary, of Adel, Georgia for her wonderful work designing the cover of this book. It is truly an inspired work of art that honors our gracious, loving Savior and God.

<u>Gene Shearl</u>: Of Valdosta, Georgia who did the photography and graphics for the cover. He is a great photographer and a genius in digital photography.

## Forward

Dr. Hendricks has a rich vein of treasured truth, knowledge, and inspiration running through the pages of this book.

It is an excellent treatment of the Ten Commandments, with strong interpretation of Scripture reinforcing and applying the laws of God to our lives.

This book deserves a place near the Book and Bible commentaries in you library.

- Dr. James N. Griffith
Executive Director
Treasurer-Emeritus
Georgia Baptist Convention

## TABLE OF CONTENTS

**Page No.**

| Page | |
|---|---|
| 8 | **Chapter 1 - Law And Grace** |
| 9 | Fulfilled By Grace |
| 16 | Binding Under Grace |
| 17 | Obeyed Through Grace |
| | |
| 18 | **Chapter 2 - Fidelity To God** |
| 20 | Numerous Are Other Gods |
| 23 | To Worship Other Gods Is Foolish |
| 24 | The Worship Of Other Gods Is Infidelity |
| 25 | Other Gods Will Disappoint |
| 28 | Other Gods Destroy |
| | |
| 31 | **Chapter 3 - Proper Worship** |
| 33 | A Proper Understanding Of God |
| 41 | The Proper Worship Of God |
| | |
| 45 | **Chapter 4 - Sincere Worship** |
| 47 | Sincerity In Reverence |
| 51 | Sincerity In Life |
| | |
| 56 | **Chapter 5 - A Day Of Worship** |
| 57 | The Integrity Of Labor |
| 61 | Time For A Day Of Rest |
| 61 | Time For A Day Of Worship |
| 63 | Time For A Day Of Commemoration |
| 64 | The Seventh Day |
| 65 | The Keeping Of The Special Day |
| 66 | Those Who Are To Keep The Day |
| | |
| 70 | **Chapter 6 - Family Obligations** |
| 60 | Obligation Of The Child To The Parent |
| 75 | Obligation Of The Parent To The Child |
| | |
| 81 | **Chapter 7 - The Sacredness Of Man's Life** |
| 81 | Murder Defined |
| 86 | God Considers Man's Life Is Sacred |
| 88 | The Definition Applied To Some Specific Cases |
| 92 | The Penalty For Murder |

| | |
|---|---|
| 93 | The Penalty For Murder Changed Under The Law |
| 95 | The Law Made Judgment For Murder More Specific |
| 96 | The Penalty Under The New Testament |
| 97 | The Penalty And God's Right To Vengeance |
| 98 | The Reasons For The Penalty |
| | |
| 105 | **Chapter 8 - Sexual Purity** |
| 106 | Sexual Purity Before |
| 110 | Sexual Purity In Marriage |
| 113 | Sexual Purity In Divorce |
| | |
| 116 | **Chapter 9 - God's Call For Honesty** |
| 116 | The Primary Source Of All Stealing |
| 118 | Secondary Sources For Stealing |
| 122 | Honesty From Man To Man |
| 126 | Honesty From Man To God |
| | |
| 132 | **Chapter 10 - A Witness For Christ Or Satan** |
| 132 | The Witnessing Power Of Man |
| 135 | Two Types Of Witness |
| 141 | Man Is To Witness To The Truth |
| | |
| 144 | **Chapter 11 - Inordinate Desires** |
| 146 | The Evil Of Inordinate Desire |
| 152 | The Destructiveness Of Inordinate Desires |
| 154 | The Way To Overcome Inordinate Desires |
| | |
| 155 | **Chapter 12 - All, Or None At All** |
| 156 | The Commandments Are Equal In Importance |
| 157 | To Violate One Commandment Is To Violate All |

# Chapter 1

## Law And Grace

(Matthew 5:17)
"Do not think that I have come to destroy the law, or the prophets: I have not come to destroy, but to complete what they started."

### - Introduction -

There are some people who deny the relevance of the Ten Commandments to present-day Christianity. What they believe is that God did away with the Law when He gave the New Testament. Their argument is that we are now living under New Testament Grace, and not under the Law.

It is true that the Apostle Paul, under the inspiration of the Holy Spirit, does say, "For by grace are you saved through faith; and not by anything that you did: *it is* the gift of God: Not of works, so that you will not be able to boast" (Ephesians 2:8-9). He also said, under the same inspiration, "For sin shall not have dominion over you: for you are not under the law, but under grace" (Romans 6:14). These quotations would seem to bear out the argument of those who would deny the value or relevance of the Ten Commandments to the Christian community of today.

But Paul also said we must not be lawless: "For we are His workmanship, created in Christ Jesus to do good works, which God has prepared ahead of time that we should do" (Ephesians 2:10).

If we have been born-again in Jesus Christ, how can we behave as lawless souls? We know the freedom that comes from the removal of the penalty of sin. We know the love of God. We know the peace of God that passes all understanding. Surely, we who are so blessed by God will be obedient to the Law of God. Surely we will accept all God's Word, including the Ten Commandments, as relevant and applicable to our lives as Christians.

We cannot, we must not, simply throw out what does not suit our fancy! We cannot, because we do not have the right to decide that some of His Word is acceptable and some of His Word may be cast aside as unacceptable. We must not, because we would lose one of the most valuable tools in our society for maintaining order and justice.

If anyone is to live by God's Law, it must be the Christian. We have had the blessings of God showered down upon us, in such a marvelous way, in our redemption through the sacrificial death of His precious Son. Day by day His blessings continue to fall on us in such great abundance. There is not a day that passes that He does not love, care for, and protect us. Being the recipients of such love should make us want to be obedient to every command of our heavenly Father, as recorded in His holy Word; if for no other reason, than simply out of gratitude and love to God.

How can we deliberately ignore God's Law and call ourselves Christian? The Apostle John, in his first epistle said, "For this is the love of God, that we obey His commandments: and His commandments are not difficult to obey" (I John 5:3). Words cannot be clearer. Christians will not deliberately ignore God's Law, but they will rejoice in it. Real, born-again children of God will seek to live by God's Law every day of their lives. It is into God's perfect Law that we find the only true guidance for a proper daily walk with Him.

James, the first pastor of the church at Jerusalem and the half brother of our Lord, states the matter in this way, "It is true, a man may say, 'You have faith, and I have works: show me your faith without any works, and I will show you my faith by my works'...Don't you understand, you foolish man, that faith which does not produce works is dead?" (James 2: 18, 20). A man who has accepted Jesus Christ by faith, and has received the grace of God in salvation is surely going to exercise that faith through obedience to, and in living by the Law of God.

In this chapter we will be discussing the relationship of the Basic Ten Laws of God to the Grace of God.

## - Fulfilled By Grace -

First, let us establish that the Grace of God fulfilled the Ten Laws, in and through the Lord Jesus Christ. In Matthew 19:16-22, Jesus tells us about a young man asking the question, "What good works shall I do, that I may earn eternal life?" This is the question of the ages. Man has said to God, "Show us how we must live, and what we must do to be right in Your sight."

What an exhibition of the pride of man! He is saying, "Let me work, and earn your love, for I am able. I know that in my own ability I am capable of pleasing You, God. In fact, I believe I can make You proud of me. Just give me the opportunity and I will show You. Let me work and earn your favor, Lord, I know that I am able."

In this we also see the arrogance of man. He was saying to his Creator, his Lord and Master, "I am strong and capable. I am smart enough to do about anything that I set my mind to. Why, look at all the accomplishments that man has achieved! We have mastered this world. We have even conquered outer space. Surely, God, you know all the things that man has accomplished in electronics; they are almost beyond comprehension. The great strides made by man in medicine are mind staggering. When one reviews all the tremendous advances man has made in the area of the arts and science, it becomes evident that we can do anything we set our minds to."

Whereas, the Bible says, "We know that a man is not justified by the works of the law, but by faith in Jesus Christ, therefore we have believed in Jesus Christ, that we might be justified by faith in Christ, and not by obeying the law: for no man can be justified by obedience to the law" (Galatians 2:16).

God dealt with that same attitude at Babel. There the people would do for themselves what was needed to preserve their existence and to show God that they were worthy of His acceptance. They said, "Let us build us a city and a tower, whose top will reach into heaven; and thereby make a name for ourselves, in case we are scattered over the face of the whole earth" (Genesis 11:4). It is obvious that their intent was also to reach God by their own efforts.

God will never tolerate such arrogance in man, because God alone is the source of all knowledge and all ability to achieve any good thing. So God said, "Consider that the people are unified; therefore nothing will be impossible for them! We must stop this from happening before they destroy themselves. If we give them different languages they will not be able to understand one another, and they will not be able to finish what they have begun" (Genesis 11:6-7).

Man further displayed his arrogance by saying to God, "I have enough goodness within myself to be acceptable in Your Kingdom. I give to charities of all kinds. I am kind to my friends and neighbors. I go to church with a fair amount of regularity, at least on Christmas, Easter, and Mother's Day. I know You must be proud of all the good things I do every day." But the prophet shows us how God see us, "We are all unclean, and all of our self-assumed righteousness is as filthy rags" (Isaiah 64:6).

The young man in Matthew 19:16-22, expresses this egotistical arrogance of mankind. The difference was he focused his argument on his ability to render total obedience: "I have been obedient to all of these from my youth" speaking of the Laws of God. He really believed he was able to be good, and do whatever else he needed to please God, because he said to Jesus, "What yet do I need?" It did not appear, at least in his own mind, that he needed anything.

He certainly was not ready for Jesus' answer: "Go sell what you have, and give to the poor, and you shall have treasure in heaven: then come follow me." He was not ready to make any real change in his life, because he did not believe he needed any change. So the Word says of him that, "he went away in great sadness: for he had great possessions." His possessions: wealth, goodness, intelligence and character should have been accepted by the Lord, or so he thought.

Here is also exhibited the sinfulness of man. He thought he was strong, and intelligent, and capable, but all he had ever shown was weakness, folly and ignorance. He thought he was good, but all he had done was evil. The Bible speaks so well concerning such an attitude:

> Now we know that the Law speaks to them who would live under the law: that every excuse of man may be stopped, and that man may see that he is guilty before God. Therefore no man can be justified in God's sight by obeying the Law: for the Law was given that we might see our sin...For all have sinned and come short of the glory of God (Romans 3:19-20, 23).
>
> As it is written, "There are none righteous, no, not one: There are none who understand, there are none who seek after God" (Romans 3:10-11).
>
> For from within, out of the heart of men, proceed evil thoughts, adulteries, fornications, murders, Thefts, covetousness, wickedness, deceit, lasciviousness, and evil eye, blasphemy, pride, foolishness: All these evil things come from within, and defile the man (Mark 7:21-23).
>
> And He said to them, "You are they who justify yourselves before men; but God knows your hearts: for that which is highly esteemed among men is abomination in the sight of God" (Luke 16:15).

Man simply does not want to recognize his dependence on God. He will not admit that he needs God for anything. He believes that he is completely self-sufficient to take care of himself and all his needs. And that attitude, without question, is sin.

So God gave man the Law. Then man got the surprise of his life. The Law was more than he could bear. Man found himself in a real dilemma. He found that he might keep some of the Law, some of the time, but he could not keep all the Law, all of the time. In fact, he could not keep some of the Law, some of the time, at least with any regularity. Paul had experienced this truth in his own life: "For the good that I want to do I do not do: but the evil things that I do not want to, they are the very things I do" (Romans 7:19).

Now man was able to see himself as he really is: sinful, weak, ignorant, and most of all lost from fellowship with God and condemned to eternity in the torment of Hell. What a predicament to find oneself in! What would he do? What could he do? Where could he turn? Was there any hope, or help? He could find none in himself.

The most painful part of this revelation was that he had brought this trouble and woe on himself. He could blame no one but himself. This was exactly the feeling that prompted the Apostle Paul to say, "O wretched man that I am! Who will deliver me from this body that would bring me death?" (Roman 7:24).

Then God came to man's rescue. God gave His precious Son to redeem man from the curse of sin. This has never been more beautifully expressed than when Jesus said, "For God loved the world so much, that He gave His only begotten Son, that whoever will believe in Him should not perish, but have everlasting life. For God sent not His Son into the world to condemn the world; but that the world through Him might be saved" (John 3:16-17).

This coming of the Son of God to earth was not like some legend of mythology. He did not come as a fully-grown man, bearing a godlike visage, and executing a godlike display of power to overwhelm and conquer the minds and hearts of men. No! He came into the world as all men come into the world. He came as a babe, born of a woman.

Oh, there was a difference in His birth from other births. He was born of a virgin, without an earthly father. God overshadowed the Virgin Mary and caused her to conceive a child without the aid of a man (Luke 1:26-38).

God, in His wisdom, knew that if the Christ came, as the product of an earthly father then He could be no Savior. If a man sired him then He would inherit the sinful nature of Adam: "Therefore, as one man caused sin to enter the world, and death entered the world because of sin; so death comes to all men, because all have sinned" (Romans 5:12). It must surely be obvious, from this, that a sinner cannot be a Savior.

Physically the Son of God was a man in every sense of the word. As we said, He was born of woman, with all the frailties of the flesh: He hungered and thirsted, just like other men. He knew weariness and exhaustion from long hours of toil and labor. He was touched by all the desires known to man. The sorrow and suffering and temptation that go with life on this earth pained him. He also knew the pangs of death. In every physical way He was a man. Yet He was fully and completely God. He bore all the weaknesses of men, but He did not succumb to the temptations and sins of this world. He did not commit sin of any kind. He did what man could not do: He kept the Law, completely, totally, and in every situation. Jesus, the incarnate Grace of God, fulfilled the Law for man. Matthew 5:17, states it plainly: "Do not think that I have come to destroy the law, or the prophets: I have not come to destroy, but to fulfill."

Jesus, by his life, death, and resurrection fulfilled the Law for man. In His life He met the demands of the Law for a perfect life. The best illustration of His meeting temptation face to face and conquering it is found in Matthew 4:1-11:

> Then Jesus was led by the Spirit into the wilderness to be tempted by the devil. And when He had fasted forty days and forty nights, afterward He was hungry. Then the tempter came to Him, and said, "If You are really the Son of God, then command that these stones to be changed to bread" But He answered and said, "It is written, 'Man shall not live by bread alone, but by every word that proceeds from the mouth of God.'" Then the devil took Him up to the holy city, and set him on a pinnacle of the temple, And said to him, "If you are the Son of God, cast yourself down: for it is written, 'He shall give his angels charge concerning you: and in their hands they will bear you up, lest at any time you dash your foot against a stone.'" Jesus said to him, "It is written again, 'You shall not tempt the Lord your God.'" Again, the devil took him up to an exceedingly high mountain, and showed him all the kingdoms of the world, and the glory of them; and said to him, "All these things will I give you, if you will fall down and worship me." Then said Jesus to him, Get away from Me, Satan: for it is written, 'Thou shall worship the Lord your God, and Him only shall you serve.'" Then the devil left him, and angels came and ministered to him.

Satan began this whole series of temptations by casting a doubt on the Sonship of Jesus. Here at the beginning of Christ's ministry, Satan tried to tempt Him to wonder if He was really doing what He was supposed to do. He wanted to make the Lord unsure of what God would have Him to do.

In the seventeenth verse of the third chapter of Matthew, we read, "And then a voice from heaven, said, 'This is my beloved Son, in whom I am well pleased.'" There on the banks of the Jordan River, following His baptism, God had confirmed the Sonship of Jesus. Now in the wilderness

Satan catches the echo of the Father's words, and began tempting where the heavenly witness ended, "If you are the Son of God, command that these stones be made bread...If you are the Son of God, cast yourself down."

Satan was trying to cast a doubt on the divinity of Jesus. Satan seldom comes to us with a point-blank denial. That would be too startling. He realizes that we might bolt and run if he was so brazen with us. He would take us by surprise. He would throw out his bait a little at a time, and draw us fully into his net before he would draw it shut. He would take his time and use much patience so as not to frighten us away. Doubt has always served the satanic purpose better than outright lies. He is more successful in his temptations by causing us to question a thing, than by a blunt denial of the truth.

Notice how Satan makes the doubt look like righteous anxiety concerning Jesus' divinity. Satan is saying, "You have a very difficult road ahead of you. Are you really sure you are up to the task? Are you sure of your strength to handle what lies ahead? Unless you are really God's Son, you will never be able to handle what you think God has given you to do. You are destined to complete failure if you have been fooled into thinking you are something that is obviously questionable." All the while Satan is making every effort to sound concerned about the welfare of the Lord.

Satan was also tempting Jesus to cater to Himself. He said to the Lord, "Command that these stones be made bread. You are hungry, so use your power to gratify your flesh. Why should you go hungry if you have all the power of God at Your disposal?"

If Satan had been successful at this point he would have destroyed our Savior. If Jesus had given in to mere bodily hunger, He would never have accepted the agonies that accompanied the trial and crucifixion. Without His willing sacrifice, there would be no salvation for sinful man.

Jesus had an answer for every temptation that Satan threw at Him. He answered Satan using the Word of God: "It is written, 'Man shall not live by bread alone, but by every word that proceeds from the mouth of God' It is written again, 'You shall not tempt the Lord your God' It is written, 'You shall worship the Lord your God, and Him only shall you serve.'" The writer of the book of Hebrews says the Word of God is, "quick, and powerful, and sharper than any two-edged sword" (Hebrews 4:12). So the Old Devil had to leave. He could not stand against the truth of God. Our Lord Jesus Christ conquered Satan for all of us who would be born-again.

It is as the writer of Hebrews said, "We have a great high priest, who is passed into the heavens, Jesus the Son of God, let us hold fast our profession. For we do not have a high priest who cannot be touched with the feeling of our infirmities; but was in all points tempted like as we are, yet without sin" (Hebrews 4:14-15). He lived the perfect life, and thereby fulfilled the Law of God.

In Luke's version of the wilderness temptation, we read that Satan "departed from him for a season" (Luke 4:13). This was certainly not Satan's last attempt to ruin our Lord. All through His ministry Satan kept trying to divert Him from His purpose. And Jesus met and answered every trial in victory. Satan could not invalidate the perfect witness of His life or His work.

The Old Serpent, called Satan, is not easily discouraged in his work. So he set out to make one final attempt to extinguish man's only hope. If he could not nullify the witness of Jesus' life, then he would annihilate Jesus. It was Satan who was behind the crucifixion and death of our Lord. Satan engineered the whole insidious plot. It was Satan in Judas Iscariot, leading in the betrayal. It was Satan in the chief priest and elders of the Jews, setting up the arrest, and mock trial, and the condemnation of Jesus. It was Satan in the multitude crying out for the release of Barabbas and the crucifixion of Jesus. Is it not amazing that mankind would choose a man who was a murderer in place of choosing a man who had only done "good" all the days of His life?

Certainly this was all in the permissive will of God. For the death of Jesus was part of the plan of God to save sinful man. God had announced this part of His plan in Genesis 3:15, when He said to the serpent, "I will put enmity between you and the woman, and between your seed and her seed; He shall bruise your head, and you shall bruise His heel." The seed of the woman, one born of a virgin without benefit of a human father, would nullify Satan's efforts to ruin God's creature, man. Satan could have done nothing unless God had allowed it to be done. Nevertheless, Satan did not know this. He thought he was destroying man's hope, not insuring it. How wonderful it is that Satan is not omniscient!

When Jesus died on the Cross, Satan really thought he had succeeded in eliminating the Son of God. When the Roman soldiers took the Lord's body down from the Cross, having determined that He was dead, Satan believed that he had succeeded in thwarting God's plans to save the world. When the body of our Lord was sealed in the tomb, Satan must have felt certain that he had succeeded in his evil plot.

But on the morning of the third day following the Christ's death and burial, Jesus conquered death and the grave. He took up His life and left the tomb, thereby offering eternal life to all who would accept His death, burial and resurrection as the sacrifice for their sin, and the answer for their justification before God.

Here was God, through Christ Jesus, doing for man what he could not do for himself. It is as Romans 8:3, says, "For what the law could not do, in that it was weak through the flesh, God sending His own Son in the likeness of sinful flesh, and for sin, condemned sin in the flesh." In the weakness of the flesh it is impossible for us to obey the Law, completely and totally, so Jesus did it for us. Now man can please God through belief in Jesus Christ: Belief in his holy life; belief that He died in our place; belief that He overcame death for us; belief that He is now interceding for us with God the Father; belief that one day He is coming to take us to live with Him forever. Romans 10:4 states it this way, "For Christ is the end of the law for righteousness to every one who believes." So Christ, the incarnate Grace of God, fulfilled the Law for man.

## - Binding Under Grace -

Even though Grace fulfilled the Ten Commandments, they are still binding under Grace. Remember, Jesus says that the Law is still in force: "Do not think that I have come to destroy the law, or the prophets: I have not come to destroy but to fulfill." He did not invalidate the Law's demand for righteousness, but He fulfilled its requirements for perfection by living the perfect life.

The Law is still here and still valid today. We read in Matthew 5:18, "Truly I say to you, until heaven and earth pass away, not even one punctuation mark shall be removed from the law, until it is all fulfilled." Until this heaven and earth give way to the New Heaven and New Earth, God's people will still be expected to keep the Law. Then we shall be perfect, and have no need of the Law to remind us how to live.

Paul says that man is saved to keep the Law: "For we are his workmanship, created in Christ Jesus to do good works, which God has before predestined that we should continue to do them" (Ephesians 2:10). This same truth is spelled out in Titus 2:14, where Paul says of Christ that He, "Gave Himself for us, that He might redeem us from all iniquity, and purify to Himself an unusual people, zealous of good works."

Listen to what Jesus says about the Christian who breaks, or teaches others to break the Law: "Whoever therefore shall break one of the least commandments, and teach other men to do also, he will be called the least in the kingdom of heaven" (Matthew 5:19). Think carefully now. If we break the Law, then by our actions we are teaching others to do the same?

Now hear what our Lord has to say about the Christian who keeps the Law and teaches others to also keep the Law of God: "But whoever shall obey the Law and teach them to others, that person shall be called great in the kingdom of heaven."

Yes, Christians are bound to keep the Law: Not to please God, not for the salvation of others, not to earn salvation for themselves, but because God wants His children to be law-abiding citizens of His Kingdom. We also should want to keep the Law, simply because we love the God and Savior who purchased our freedom from sin, and thereby gave us the ability to keep the Law.

## - Obeyed Through Grace -

To this some may say, "But I thought you have been saying that a man cannot keep the Law?" That is true, but only so far as concerning the lost; those outside the Grace of God. But it is not true concerning the saved in Christ Jesus. The Ten Commandments can be obeyed through Grace.

Jesus says He gives us the power, to keep the Law, if we abide in Him: "I am the vine, you are the branches, He that abides in me, and I in him, the same brings forth much fruit: for without me you can do nothing" (John 15:5). Actually, whatever good we may do is done in and through us by Jesus Christ. We must allow Him to come into our lives and possess them completely if we are to be successful in keeping the Law, or, for that matter, if we are to be successful in anything else.

Paul says, in II Corinthians 9:8, "God is able to make all grace abound toward you; that you, always having all sufficiency in all things, may abound to every good work." In other words, God's grace is sufficient for all things. God's Grace is the means to the fulfillment of the Law.

# Chapter 2

## Fidelity To God

(Exodus 20:3)
"You shall have no other gods before Me."

### - Introduction -

Having prepared the way for the study of the Ten Commandments by considering their relationship to Grace, we are now ready to take up the Ten Laws individually.

There is an old saying that is most applicable to this part of our study: "First Things First." It is possible to study the Ten Commandments, beginning with any one of the Ten, but there is much to be lost in doing so. The best place to begin a study of the Ten Laws of God is with the First Commandment.

One day, following His Triumphal Entry, Jesus was teaching a great multitude in the Temple. During the discourse He was approached by a Pharisee, a teacher of the Law, who asked Him, "Master, which is the great commandment in the law?" (Matthew 22:36). To which Jesus replied, "'you shall love the Lord your God with all your heart, and with all your soul, and with all your mind.' This is the first and great commandment" (Matthew 22:37-38). He was expounding the truth that this commandment not only came first in the listing, but also first in importance, and was intended to be first in obedience. This is true because the ability to obey the other nine Laws hinge on obedience to this first and foremost commandment. Until man puts God in first place in his life he will find himself unable to be obedient in other things. Therefore man's gravest danger lies in disobedience to this commandment.

The First Commandment is also primary because Man's propensity to worship something makes it primary. Within the soul of man is a desire to have and love a god. This desire is part of the nature of man. This is true because when the Lord God created man He put this desire in him. In the great heart of God was the desire for man to seek after Him and to find Him. God wanted man to come to Him for fellowship and love. But God made no dictates concerning man's choice of a god, only that he would desire one. God does not want man as a puppet on a string, to manipulate this way and that way. God does not want man to come to Him by force or coercion, but freely and of his own desire.

We see the truth of this when God placed Adam and Eve in the Garden of Eden. He had created the Garden a paradise with everything they could have desired: plenty of food, and that of the best and tastiest kind; a perfect climate in which to live; a loving God to watch over them and to provide all that they needed (Genesis 2:8-16).

God made only one prohibition for them. They must not eat of the fruit of the tree of the knowledge of good and evil, which was in the midst of the garden. God made it clear that they did not need that one tree; for in Him and His provisions for them there was sufficiency. He also warned them that to eat of the fruit of that tree would bring death to them (Genesis 2:17). He was simply saying to them, "In Me you will find all that you will ever need, but you must choose to serve Me freely and without reservation or rival."

In the tree of the knowledge of good and evil was wrapped up all that man could desire in the world: knowledge, talent, beauty, power, prestige, and wealth. However, there were two undesirables included in that package: limited existence in the world, and eternal separation from God in the world to come. In God was wrapped up all that man could desire or need for this world: wisdom, peace, joy, fellowship with Him and His children, and all of the other things worthwhile and necessary, and eternal life with Him in the world to come. Man was thereby given a choice, and would therefore be accountable for his choice.

Adam and Eve made their choice in choosing to eat of the tree of which God said, "You shall not eat of it: for in the day that you eat thereof you shall surely die" (Genesis 2:17). Having done so, they could not blame God for the problems they faced. God had warned them, but they chose not to listen to Him. Now sentence was passed on them because of their choice.

To Eve God said:
> I will greatly multiply your sorrow and your conception; in sorrow you shall bring forth children; and your desire *shall* be to your husband, and he shall rule over you (Genesis 3:16).

To Adam God said:
> Because you have listened to the voice of your wife, and have eaten of the tree, of which I commanded you, saying, "You shall not eat of it: cursed is the ground for your sake; in sorrow shall you eat of it all the days of your life; Thorns also and thistles shall it bring forth to you; and you shall eat the herb of the field; In the sweat

of your face you shall eat bread, until you return to the ground; for out of it were you taken: for dust you are, and to dust you shall return (Genesis 3:17-19).

They made the choice. They had to pay the price. So it shall be with every man who holds to other gods, to worship and serve. It would be safer to hold a deadly serpent to ones breast.

## - Numerous Are Other Gods -

Nevertheless, man has continuously held other gods in reverence, worshipping almost anything and everything that comes to eye or mind. You name it and man has or is worshipping it. These gods, without exception, are the creation of man's mind. For anything that is loved more than all else, by the mind and heart of a man, becomes a god to that man. That is the making of a god: the giving of total reverence to an object; the complete subjection of ones total being to something or some person.

Man has made a god of money, or so it is true when he gives all his time and effort in storing it up. When money, or the accumulation of money, is the all-consuming passion, then it has become a god. When man has no time for family because he must make more money, then money has become his god. When a man can think of nothing else but money, it has become his god. Hosea 8:4, says, "Of their silver and their gold have they made to themselves idols."

Today this is truer of the accumulation of money than of the casting of molten idols, but it makes the accumulation of money no less the idol that is worshipped by man. Such a man is like King Midas, who found his greatest pleasure in handling and fondling his accumulated wealth. Also, like Midas, their great desire is for everything they touch to turn to gold.

Property can become just as much a god as money. There is a pleasure that goes along with the accumulation of property that is just as engrossing and possessing as the worship of a god. In Matthew 22:5, Jesus tells the parable of the wedding feast, and speaks to this same subject when He tells of the excuses those invited make for not coming: "But they made light of the invitation and went their ways, one to his farm, another to his merchandise." Their property was more important to them than obedience to the command of the king. Perhaps the farmer needed to check his crops to see how bountiful they were going to be. It could be that the merchant was taking inventory. It really does not matter what they were doing, because nothing should have been more important than obedience to their king. In their minds and hearts they had placed their property above their king. Their property had become their king and god.

Jesus tells us the same thing, in His parable of the man who prepared a great supper and invited many to come. It is recorded in Luke 14:18, where one made an excuse for not attending the supper by saying, "I have bought a piece of ground, and it need to go and see it." Another made the same type of excuse when he said, in verse 19, "I have bought five yoke of oxen, and I go to prove them." Can you imagine any man buying a piece of ground or a yoke of oxen without first seeing what he was getting for his money? Of course not! They knew what they had bought. What kept them from going to the supper was their worship of property. Their property had become their god. They must continually adore it. They must feast their eyes on it constantly. Their property had become more important than any other thing, so it became their god.

It is sad when men make gods of human beings, because it is only a step away from self-worship. It is true, however, that men do make gods out of other human beings. In the same parable of the great supper, Luke 14:20, Jesus tells of another man's excuse for not attending the feast, he said, "I have married a wife, and therefore I cannot come." His wife was more important, to him, then all other things so she became his god.

I saw this same kind of worship, one time, in the home of a couple in which I was visiting. As I entered the living room of that home I was struck by the beauty of what was obviously an altar, or a shrine just above the piano. On the wall over the piano was the picture of a beautiful child. On each end of the piano top was a lamp with its beam directed onto the picture of the child. I asked the couple, "Is this your daughter?" In reverent tones they said that it was.

Then they told me how she had died. It was obvious, however, that she was just as alive in their minds as if she had stood physically in front of them at that moment. It was also obvious that they had made her their god, and this shrine was their altar of worship, and the portrait was their image to worship. Their little dead girl had become their god, for they had made her such in their minds.

Power becomes a mighty god in the lives of some people. Look at the dictators who have fed their souls with a lust for power. They worship at the altar of power. It is their God.

To others entertainment has become a god. They pursue it with an intensity that defies expression. It is one party after another; one movie after another, one novel after another. On and on and on it goes. They fill their time with nothing else, or at least that is what they would do if they could. Nothing is more important than that their appetite for entertainment be satisfied.

One great god of this nation is the god of sports. Sports take up more time and thought than almost anything else. It is drilled into the heads of our school children that there is nothing more important.

In one town in which I lived football had become more important than the education of the children. When the football coach, who was one of the best in the state, had a run-in with the principal, who was doing a fantastic job academically, the School Board moved the principal out. Football was more important. Football had become the god of some of the citizens of that town.

The god of sex is held up daily before our eyes for our worship. It is Satan's hope that we will accept it as our god. There are many for whom it has become a god. They dress according to its dictates. They order their lives after its will. It is their all-consuming passion. It is the god they worship and adore, and pornographic literature is their sacred scripture on faith and practice.

Down through the centuries men have made a god out of religion. That is what the Pharisees of Jesus' day did. They had forgotten whom they were to worship, and made the practices and forms of worship their god. The rituals were more important than God for whom the rituals were made to honor; therefore the rituals became the god.

In Matthew 15:1-9, Jesus dealt with this kind of idolatry:

> Then came to Jesus scribes and Pharisees, who were from Jerusalem, saying, "Why do your disciples transgress the tradition of the elders? For they do not wash their hands when they eat bread." But He answered and said to them, "Why do you also transgress the commandment of God by your tradition? For God commanded, saying, 'Honor your father and mother: and, He who curses father or mother, let him die the death.' But you say, "Whoever shall *say* to his father or his mother, '*It is* a gift, by whatever you may be profited by me'; and does not honor his father or his mother, *he shall be free*." This way you have made the commandment of God void by your tradition. You hypocrites, well did Isaiah prophesy of you, saying, "This people draws near to me with their mouth, and honor me with *their* lips; but their heart is far from me. But in vain they are worshipping me, teaching *for* doctrines the commandments of men.'"

If we are not careful, we can make our forms of worship our god instead of the Lord God. What a shame to disobey the Lord God's commandment by worshipping the forms of worship instead of the God they were intended to glorify and honor.

There are also those who try to serve other gods and the Lord God at the same time. They are those who are going to cover all sides of a situation. They are the ones who would say, "Why take chances? We will serve the Lord God too. If He is real, then we will be all right. If He is not real, it will not matter. We will be safe either way." There is neither safety nor satisfaction in this. Matthew 6:24, says, "No man can serve two masters: for either he will hate the one, and love the other; or else he will hold to the one, and despise the other. You cannot serve God and money."

The New Samaritans, who were transplanted by the King of Assyria in the land of Israel, found this to be true. When they arrived in the land they continued to serve other gods, as they had been accustomed to do. II Kings 17:25, 32-33, says:

> And so it was at the beginning of their dwelling there, *that* they did not fear the Lord: therefore the Lord sent lions among them, which slew *some* of them...So they feared the Lord, and made for themselves of the lowest of them priests of the houses of the high places. They feared the Lord, and served their own gods, after the manner of the nations from which they were carried away.

The "Better Safe Than Sorry" policy will not work with God. Moses said in Deuteronomy 4:24, "For the Lord your God is a consuming fire, even a jealous God." He will not tolerate sharing you with other gods. God said in II Kings 17:35, "You shall not fear other gods, nor bow yourselves to them, nor serve them, nor sacrifice to them." He has also commanded, "You shall have no other gods before me" (Exodus 20:3). That means not only in place of, but also with or at the same time. He will have all your love and service or none at all. He will not allow you to share your service with another god or gods.

## - To Worship Other Gods Is Foolish -

When God said, "You shall have no other gods before me," He was literally saying, "To have other gods is foolish, because they are created things. Whether they are in the heavens above or in the earth below; He made them all."

God is telling us that it is foolish to worship other gods because they are powerless as gods. Can they speak anything into being? Can they darken the sun? Can they calm the angry sea? Can they heal the sick or make the blind to see or the deaf to hear or the dumb to speak or the lame to walk? Can they raise the dead? Can they give you eternal life? The answer is obvious: They cannot. Only the Lord God, the Almighty, can do such things.

One does not have to think too deeply to see that gods created out of created things are gods that will perish. The stars fall, the sun is dying, wood rots, stone erodes, metals rust, even man is as "a vapor that appears for a little while and then vanishes away" (James 4:14). How can we worship such temporary things? Worship only Him who is worthy of worship: The Self-existent, Eternal God. God is, always has been, and always will be. For Him there is no beginning nor ending. To worship Him is wisdom of the highest order.

## - The Worship Of Other Gods Is Infidelity -

Again God is saying, "To have other gods is infidelity." This is certainly true for the Christian. Because we have been purchased by the blood of God's precious Son Jesus. Jesus did not die on the Cross, paying the price to redeem man, so that the man He had redeemed could worship other gods. We cannot expect Him to say, "Oh that is all right. I do not mind sharing My redeemed with other gods." What He is actually saying is, "Worshipping other gods is purely and simply infidelity, and I will not tolerate it."

It is also infidelity because we that are saved are part of the bride of Christ. Therefore to have other gods is spiritual adultery. Paul states it this way,

> And what agreement has the temple of God with idols? For you are the temple of the living God; as God has said "I will dwell in them, and walk in *them*; and I will be their God, and they shall be my people. Wherefore come out from among them, and be separate," says the Lord, "and do not touch the unclean *thing*; and I will receive you" (II Corinthians 6:16-17).

It is also infidelity for the lost to serve other gods. God, likewise, created them, therefore, they belong to Him. It is infidelity for the creature to worship anything, or anyone, other than the Creator:

> For the wrath of God is revealed from heaven against all ungodliness and unrighteousness of men, who hold the truth in unrighteousness; Because that which may be known of God is manifest in them; for God has shown *this* to them. For the invisible things of Him from the creation of the world are clearly seen, being under-

stood by the things that are made, *even* His eternal power and Godhead; so that they are without excuse: Because that, when they knew God, they glorified *Him* not as God, neither were thankful; but became vain in their imaginations, and their foolish heart was darkened. Professing themselves to be wise, they became fools, and changed the glory of the incorruptible God into an image made like to corruptible man, and to birds, and four-footed beasts, and creeping things. Wherefore God also give them up to uncleanness through the lusts of their own hearts, to dishonor their own bodies between themselves: Who changed the truth of God into a lie, and worshiped and served the creature more than the Creator, who is blessed forever. Amen (Romans 1:18-25).

## - Other Gods Will Disappoint -

It is obvious that the love that creates other gods is a love of selfishness and greed. It is the pleasing of self and the desires of self that is the material from which all other gods are fashioned. Therefore they are unholy gods, lustful gods, and evil gods. So in essence they are gods that will disappoint.

Anything made to be a god by the mind of man must be, at best, an extremely imperfect god. They are gods that cannot be trusted. They are gods that will let men down when needed most. The truth of this is seen in Jezebel's god, Baal.

Jezebel had built her whole life on the worship of Baal (I Kings 29-32). When she married Ahab, the king of Israel, she brought Baal worship with her. As the High Priestess of Baal worship she intended that the people of Israel would worship Baal. Baal must be the leading god, and it did not make any difference to Jezebel what she had to do for this to happen. She would lie, cheat, steal, and murder to accomplish her goal. She believed in the power of Baal, or at least the power that she possessed as the High Priestess of Baal worship. You see she really worshipped two gods. She worshiped Baal, and she worshiped power. Of course Baal was only the outward manifestation of her real object of worship: Power.

Elijah, the prophet of the Lord God, knew all about Jezebel's god, Baal. Elijah knew that there was no substance to such a god. He knew that Baal was the creation of man's mind. So he challenged the prophets of Baal to a test. He challenged them to prove that Baal existed other than in their minds.

In I Kings 18:25, we find the challenge: "And Elijah said to the prophets of Baal, Choose bullock for yourselves, and dress it first; for you are many; and call on the name of your gods, but put no fire under your sacrifice." Elijah was simply saying, "Show me if your god is real or imagined. If he is real he should be able to consume a sacrifice from off the altar without any help from you. Let us see if he can. If so it will prove that he is a god worthy of worship."

The prophets of Baal built their altar according to their custom. Then they took a bull and killed it and cut it up after the fashion of Baal worship and placed all the pieces on the altar. They did everything just so. Then they began to call on the name of their god. They performed every ritualistic gesture. They danced their pagan dances, whirling and gyrating to their heathen music. They chanted and prayed every prayer that they knew. From morning until noon they did this, but no answer came. The sacrifice remained on their altar just as they had placed it.

All the while Elijah was watching and laughing inside. He must have been laughing because he began to mock them saying, "Cry aloud for he is a god; either he is talking or off hunting, or on a journey, or perhaps he is asleep and must be awakened" (I Kings 18:27).

Elijah was enjoying every minute of their embarrassment. These prophets of Baal had hurt the Children of Israel with their insidious plots to draw them into Baal worship. It is not difficult to understand Elijah's pleasure at the obvious showing of Baal's impotence. It was just too good to pass up the opportunity to make them look as foolish as possible.

Well, Elijah succeeded in making them terribly uncomfortable, and they began to show their irritation. They began to scream and shout at Baal until it must have appeared that Baal was hard of hearing. When that brought no results they began to mutilate their bodies with knives to show their devotion to Baal. The blood covered their bodies and dripped off onto the ground, but still no answer came to encourage them. What a disappointment their god Baal must have been to those prophets. Their god had failed them completely, leaving them in utter humiliation.

As it was with Baal, so it will be with all gods created by the mind of man. They must and will ultimately disappoint those who have created them. Such gods are powerless to affect those who worship them, other than to bring evil and disappointment upon them. The final result upon the worshiper of such gods is devastating.

Naaman, the leprous soldier of Syria (II Kings 5:1-19), found the truth of this when money failed to be a god of trust and confidence. He had really believed that money could do all things, if one spread enough of it around.

On a raid into the land of Israel, Naaman and his army had taken captives and returned to Syria. Among the captives was a little girl whom Naaman gave to his wife to be her servant. Evidently Naaman and his wife were kindhearted people, for the maid was concerned about her master's condition. One day she said to her mistress, "Would God my lord was with the prophet that is in Samaria! For he would heal him of his leprosy."

When Naaman heard that he could be cured of his leprosy in the Land of Israel, he took a vast amount of money and many precious treasures and headed for Samaria. He felt certain that these things would be needed as payment for the miracle he needed to be performed. Money was his cure for all problems. At least he thought that money was the answer.

This time he was in for a terrible disappointment, because his money was no help. If he would be cured it must be done according to the Lord God of Elisha. What a disappointment the "god of money" was to Naaman.

If you have created for yourself a god of property, it will also fail you. Many that lived in the twenties and thirties during the Great Depression testify to this truth. They amassed large amounts of property. They were sure that no matter what happened, their god of property would keep them secure from all problems and troubles. In their minds they knew that money might become worthless, but land would always be needed and therefore it would always be valuable. This sounds so much like the men in Isaiah's day about whom God said, "Woe to those who join house to house, who add field to field, until there is no place left for others, they will be left alone in the middle of the earth!" (Isaiah 5:8). Then came the Depression. Land values dropped to nearly nothing, and so did the value of money. All was lost. Their god had failed them, as all gods created by the minds of men must do.

If power is the god you seek after to serve and worship, it too will fail you. Power is a fickle god at best. Its favors are fleeting. This is attested to by the kings and dictators who have made power their god: Pharaoh, Alexander the Great, Nero, and Hitler. They are all gone from this life, and so is the power they possessed. Search the annals of history and you will see that the god of power has, and always will disappoint.

There is only one true and living God, and He never fails or disappoints. The Lord God, the Ruler of Heaven and earth, is always faithful and true to those who worship and adore Him. He is always by our side when we need Him. He never lets us down.

After Baal had failed so miserably as a god, Elijah told the prophets of Baal that it was his turn. The story is recorded in I Kings 18:31-38. Elijah took twelve stones, one for each of the twelve tribes of Israel, and built an altar in the name of the Lord. Then he made a trench around the altar, and called for four barrels of water to be poured over the sacrifice. He then called for four more barrels of water, and poured them over the sacrifice. Then once more he called for another four barrels of water and poured them over the sacrifice; which made twelve in all. By this time the sacrifice was soaked, so was the wood under the sacrifice, and the trench around the altar was filled with water. Everything was now ready.

At the proper time for the evening sacrifice Elijah approached the altar and said, "Lord God of Abraham, Isaac, and of Israel, let it be known this day that You alone are God in Israel, and that I am your servant, and that I have done all these things according to your word. Hear me, O Lord, hear me, that this people may know that You are the Lord God, and that You have turned their heart back again." No sooner had he said the last word of his prayer than fire from God rained out of heaven and consumed the sacrifice, the wood, the stones, and the water in the trench. Nothing was left. Most of all there was no doubt left in the heart of anyone present concerning who was the true God, and who was the prophet of the true God.

Naaman found this to be true. When he forgot his god of money and became obedient to the Lord God, he was healed. Certainly it was not easy to dip himself seven times in the muddy water of the River Jordan, but he was willing to do whatever God wanted him to do when his god failed him. Now he could go home cured of his leprosy, and with a new God who would never fail him.

## - Other Gods Destroy -

Yes, gods created by the minds of men will be gods that will disappoint. But worse than that, they will be gods that will destroy those who worship them. Notice again the prophets of Baal. After the failure of Baal on Mount Carmel, all four hundred of the prophets of Baal were slain. Not one of them was left to practice this evil in the land of Israel. We are told that Elijah slew them, and so he did, but actually it was their service to a false god that did them in. It will do it every time.

Jezebel found this to be true, even though it did take some twenty years for it to catch up with her:

> And when Jehu came to Jezreel, Jezebel heard of *his arrival*; and she painted her face, and arranged her hair, and looked out of a window. And as Jehu entered in at the gate, she said, "*Had* Zimri peace, who slew his master?" And he lifted up his face to the window, and said, "Who is on my side? Who?" And there looked out to him two *or* three eunuchs. And he said, "Throw her down." So they threw her down: and *some* of her blood

was sprinkled on the wall, and on the horses: and he trampled her under foot (II Kings 9:30-33).

Later Jehu decided that since she was a queen she should at least have a burial, and he sent servants to do the job. When they went to get her body, they found that the dogs had eaten all but her skull, and feet, and the palms of her hands; which fulfilled the prophecy of Elijah concerning Jezebel's death (I Kings 21:23).

Here Jehu was the avenging hand of the Lord God, but it was still because she had chosen to worship and serve a false god.

Other gods never fail to destroy those who serve them. This can be seen to be true in the life of Gehazi, the servant of Elisha (II Kings 5:20-27). You will recall that Elisha had refused Naaman's money for using the power of God to cure him of leprosy. But behind Elisha's back Gehazi followed Naaman and took two talents of silver and two changes of garments and hid them in his house. He thought he had done a good days work for his god of money. He did not know it but he was about to reap his wages for his service to other gods.

When Gehazi went in and stood before Elisha, his master asked him where he had been. He answered, "I have not been any where at all." He could not lie to the man of God. Elisha told him that he knew where he had been, and said to him "The leprosy of Naaman shall cling to you, and to your descendants forever." Gehazi went out from his presence a leper as white as snow. Other gods always take their toll.

Ananias and Sapphira worshipped the god of money. They also found that other gods destroy those who worship them (Acts 5:1-11). When the Jerusalem church was first begun, everybody sold what they had and gave the money into the treasury of the church. In this way everyone in the fellowship was taken care of according to their needs. Ananias and Sapphira sold their property, but they gave only a portion of the money to the apostles. When Peter asked Ananias if what they had given was all the money, he said that it was. Peter asked him why he was lying to the Holy Spirit. Immediately Ananias fell dead at Peter's feet.

Later Ananias' wife, Sapphira, came in and Peter asked her the same question and she also lied. Just then Peter heard the men returning who had carried the body of Ananias out. When he told Sapphira who was coming, she too fell dead. So they carried her out and buried her with her husband. The false gods created by the minds of men, and worshiped in their hearts, will always destroy the worshipers.

The Rich Farmer of Jesus' parable, in Luke 12:16-21, is probably the best example of a man serving the god of property and paying the penalty of that service. He had enough property that he thought he would never want for anything. His property would take care of his every need. But the Lord God said that he was a fool, because he was going to die that night. All of his property could not help him. Jesus in commenting on this said, "So is he that stores up treasure for himself, and is not rich toward God" (Luke 12:21).

There was a man from the city of Samaria named Simon, a magician of some renown, who learned about worshiping other gods (Acts 8:9-21). His god was power. He was always looking for new powers to keep the people in awe of him. One day he saw the apostles Peter and John laying hands on some new converts and thereby bestowing on them the Holy Spirit. When he saw the results of the receiving of the Holy Spirit, he offered Peter money to tell him how he could have that power. Peter's answer is sufficient proof that other gods will destroy those who worship them: "Your money will perish with you, because you thought that the gift of God may be purchased with money" (Acts 8:20).

It is clear from this study that when God said, "You shall have no other gods before me," He meant it in the most serious way. Therefore, we should keep that seriousness in mind and be obedient to it in Christ Jesus the Lord. If we are in Christ Jesus, our love for Him should make such obedience the joy of our lives.

# Chapter 3

## Proper Worship

(Exodus 20:4)
"You shall not make for yourself any carved image."

### - Introduction -

In the last chapter we spoke about fidelity to God. Over and over again He has said that He will not share His people with any other god. He must be their only God. So He said, "You shall not serve or worship any other god." Likewise He must have all His people's love and service. He is explicitly emphatic about this.

Moses expressed this truth repeatedly:

> Hear, O Israel: The Lord our God *is* one Lord: And you shall love the Lord your God with all your heart, and with all your soul, and with all your might (Deuteronomy 6:4-5).

> And now, Israel, what does the Lord your God require of you, but to fear the Lord your God, to walk in all His ways, and to love Him, and serve the Lord your God with all your heart and with all your soul, To keep the commandments of the Lord, and His statutes, which I command you this day for your good? (Deuteronomy 10:12-13).

> Therefore you shall love the Lord your God, and keep His demands, and his statutes, and his judgments, and his commandments, always...you shall listen carefully to my commandments which I command you this day, to love the Lord your God, and to serve him with all your heart and with all your soul...you shall thoroughly keep all these commandments which I command you, to do them, to love the Lord your God, to walk in all his ways, and to cling to Him (Deuteronomy 11:1, 13, 22).

> If there arise among you a prophet, or a dreamer of dreams, who gives you a sign or a wonder, And the sign

or the wonder come to pass, whereof he spoke to you, saying, Let us go after other gods, which you have not known, and let us serve them; You shall not listen to the words of that prophet, or that dreamer of dreams: for the Lord your God testing you, to see whether you love the Lord your God with all your heart and with all your soul (Deuteronomy 13:1-3).

Joshua picked up the words of Moses and said to Israel:

But be very careful to obey the commandment and the law, which Moses the servant of the Lord delivered to you, to love the Lord your God, and to walk in all His ways, and to keep His commandments, and to hold fast to him, and to serve Him with all your heart and with all your soul (Joshua 22:5).

Jesus, as the living God incarnate, verifies that Moses and Joshua were right to stress this truth when He answered the lawyer's question about which commandment was the greatest by quoting from them:

The first of all the commandments is, "Hear, O Israel; The Lord our God is one Lord: And you shall love the Lord your God with all your heart, and with all your soul, and with all your mind, and with all your strength: this is the first commandment (Mark 12:29-30).

Now we come to the Second of the Ten Commandments:

You shall not make for yourself any graven image, or any likeness *of any thing* that *is* in heaven above, or that *is* in the earth beneath, or that *is* in the water under the earth: You shall not bow before them, nor serve them: for I the Lord your God *am* a jealous God, visiting the iniquity of the fathers on the children to the third and fourth *generation* of them that hate Me; and showing mercy to thousands of them that love Me, and keep My commandments (Exodus 20:4-6).

Just what is prohibited by this commandment? Does it prohibit portraits of our families and ourselves? Does it prohibit the pictures with which we decorate the walls of our homes? Does this forbid the great works of art: the landscapes, the animal and bird life works, the subjects inspired by the Old and New Testaments that were done by the genius of Rembrandt; or the marvelous sculpture of Aguste Rodin, and Michelangelo; or the Impressionistic paintings of Claude Monet? Thank God, it does not! What a loss it would be to the people of this world if it were so! God gave these artists their marvelous talent to honor Him and to bless mankind. The Command is that we are not to worship such things. We are not to bow down to them or serve them.

This is not a repetition of the First Commandment, even though there are some who believe that it is. Actually this Commandment concerns the proper worship of God, not the worship of false gods.

What we really find in this Second Commandment is two lessons that must be learned if we are to properly observe this law: The first is that we must have a proper understanding of God. The second is that we must learn the proper way to worship God.

## - A Proper Understanding Of God -

Now, the question is "Can we really understand God?" I believe that we can. I further believe that God wants man to understand Him. If this were not so then why did God give us a commandment that demands that we learn a proper understanding of Him? Why give a revelation at all? It is obvious that God gave us His Word that we may know Him. Why would God send His Son Jesus to earth if it were not intended for us to understand Him? When in fact John 1:18, tells us that this is the primary reason Jesus came to earth: "No man has seen God at any time; but the only Son of God, who is very close to the Father, He has made Him known." Jesus also emphasizes this truth to the twelve apostles in John 14:7-11:

> If you had known me, you should have known my Father also: and from now on you will know him, because you have seen him. Philip said to Him, "Lord, show us the Father, and it will satisfy us." Jesus said to him, "Have I been such a long time with you, and yet you still do not know Me, Philip? He that has seen Me has seen the Father; and how can you *then* say, 'Show us the Father?' Do you not believe that I am in the Father, and the Father in me? The words that I speak to you I speak not of Myself: but the Father that dwells in Me, He does the works. Believe Me that I *am* in the Father, and the Father in Me: or else believe Me for the very works' sake.

Man has ever had a desire to see and know God. This desire ties in directly with man's need to worship a god. In the previous chapter, we said that God placed this need in the soul of man. He wanted man to need a god to worship and serve. But He wanted it to be Himself and no other god, and He made it a law that it must be so: "You shall have no other gods before me."

Down through the centuries man has been saying, "I want to see the god I worship and serve." This is so because man has generally been taught that one is to believe little if anything that he hears, and almost nothing that he reads. To man the only real test of truth is what he can see and feel and taste. Therefore, his desire is to have a material expression of his god. He wants to know his god from a physical experience: by sight and touch. At the least he desires a personal knowledge of his god: an experimental knowledge of the god he worships.

Moses expressed this same desire when he said to God:

> See, You say to me, "Bring up this people: and You have not let me know whom You will send with me. Yet You have said, "I know you by name, and you have also found grace in my sight." Now therefore, I pray You, if I have found grace in Your sight, show me now your way, that I may know You, that I may find grace in Your sight: and consider that this nation is Your people (Exodus 33:12-13).

So God said to Moses, "My presence shall go with you, and I will give you rest" (Exodus 33:14). Can there be any question that Moses wanted to know God, or that God wanted Moses to know Him?

This desire was at the heart of what Elijah wanted when he ran from Jezebel. He really felt forsaken, for he said, "I have been very jealous for the Lord God of hosts: for the children of Israel have forsaken Your covenant, thrown down Your altars, and slain Your prophets with the sword; and I, even I only, am left; and they seek my life to take it away" (I King 19:10).

Here again God responded in a positive way, to Elijah, as He did with Moses:

> Go forth, and stand on the mountain before the Lord. And, behold, the Lord passed by, and a great and strong wind rent the mountains, and broke in pieces the rocks before the Lord; *but* the Lord *was* not in the wind: and after the wind an earthquake; *but* the Lord *was* not in the earthquake: And after the earth quake a fire; *but* the Lord *was* not in the fire: and after the fire a still small voice (I Kings 19:11-12).

In this most graphic way God explained to Elijah that the physical is really of small importance; what counts is His presence in the "still small voice" of His Word. He is always present with us in His Word.

On the night before He was crucified, Jesus said to the Apostles, "If you had known me, you should have known my Father also: and from now on you will know Him, because you have seen Him" (John 14:6-7). The

Apostle Philip simply could not understand this, so he expressed this age-old desire of man: "Lord, show us the Father, and it will satisfy us." To which Jesus responded, "Have I been such a long time with you, and yet you still do not know Me, Philip? He who has seen Me has seen the Father; and how can you then say, 'Show us the Father?'" (John 14:8-9).

You see, there is no harm in the desire to know and understand God. This is obvious when we see over and over again that God has manifested Himself to man in response to the expression of this desire. The harm comes when man lets his desire run away with him. This was the problem of Israel at Mount Sinai. Moses had gone up on the mountain to meet with God. We are told in Exodus 24:18, that "Moses was on the mountain forty days and forty nights." Evidently the days had dragged by, and the people became restless, for it says in Exodus 32:1:

> And when the people saw that Moses delayed coming down from the mountain, they gathered themselves around Aaron, and said to him, Go, make us gods, which shall go before us; as for this Moses, the man that brought us up out of the land of Egypt, we do not know what has become of him.

They had been forbidden to go near the mountain, so they could not see God or talk to Him. Moses, the nearest contact they had with God, was gone. After all this time they probably thought that he had fallen from a cliff and been killed. So instinct took over, and they wanted a god they could see, worship, serve and follow. Nothing else or less would do. Here the desire got out of control and led to sin:

> And the Lord said to Moses, "Go, get yourself down; for your people, which you brought out of the land of Egypt, have corrupted themselves: They have turned aside quickly from the way which I commanded them: they have made a molten calf, and have worshiped it, and have sacrificed to it, and said, 'This *is* your god, O Israel, which has brought you out of the land of Egypt (Exodus 32:7-8).

They disobeyed the Second Commandment.

So it has ever been. Man has let his desire to see the god he worships lead him astray. He wants something tangible to look on and kneel before. The desire to see his god has led men to make graven images.

Look at the worship Paul found at Athens: (Acts 17:22-31). There it is made patently plain what man's desire to see the god he worships will lead him into. These Athenians had gods for every situation, and therefore of almost everything. They even had an altar for "THE UNKNOWN GOD."

They wanted to be sure they did not slight any god. The King James Version has Paul saying that they were too superstitious." Actually he was saying that they were too religious. They had so much religion that the practice of religion, itself, had actually become their god. Paul said that God had put up with this until He sent Jesus into the world, but now that Christ has come, God will allow this practice no longer. Now man must leave his gods, the graven images, and repent and turn to Christ Jesus for salvation.

Things have not changed much since Paul's day. Men still have their graven images and idols. We even see this in some religions that are part of the "Christian Community." They have statues of those they call saints, and statues of the Virgin Mary, and statues of Christ. Mostly this latter takes the form of a Crucifix: the carved figure of Christ nailed to the Cross (even if it were all right to have images of the one we worship, this is still wrong because we do not worship a crucified Christ but a risen Savior). At best this is the fulfilling of the desire to see a physical manifestation of the one worshipped. At the worst it is idolatry. God said, "You shall not make for yourself any carved image, or any likeness of anything...You shall not bow down to them..."

The reason for this blatant disregard of God's command against graven images is a lack of understanding of God. When men get a proper understanding of God, they lose the desire for an image of Him whom they worship: they find they have no need for an image. So let us be obedient to this Commandment and learn the truth about God.

The first thing that we must learn about God is that He is not flesh and blood; He is Spirit. Jesus tells us this in John's Gospel: "God is a Spirit..." (John 4:24a). Actually, according to the original language, the article "a" should not be in the verse. It should read, "God is Spirit," as "God is love" (I John 4:8), and "God is light" (I John 1:5).

If God is Spirit, then He is invisible to the physical eye of man. We cannot conceive a mental picture of God, because we of necessity must put flesh on all beings, even God, to create a picture of them. If God is Spirit, He has no flesh; therefore, we cannot make a true physical representation of God. There is no image that can be made of the invisible God.

Perhaps you are asking the question, "What about Christ being the express image of the Father?" Scripture does teach this truth. We are told in John 1:1, "In the beginning was the Word, and the Word was with God, and the Word was God." The fourteenth verse of the same chapter says, "And the Word was made flesh, and dwelt among us, (and we beheld his glory, the glory as of the only begotten of the Father,) full of grace and truth." The writer of the book of Hebrews sums it up with the identical words of the question:

God, who at various times and in different ways spoke in time past to the fathers by the prophets, Has in these last days spoken to us by His Son, whom he has appointed heir of all things, by whom also He made the worlds; who being the brightness of His glory, and the express image of His person, and upholding all things by the word of his power, when he had by himself purged our sins, sat down on the right hand of the Majesty on high (Hebrews 1:1-3).

It is also true that Jesus said, "He that has seen me has seen the Father" (John 14:9). So there is no doubt that Christ is the image of the Father. It is true that Scripture does teach that Jesus came to show us the Father. However, none of the above passages of Scripture, or any other passages of Scripture is speaking of image in the sense that man conceives of image. It is certainly not speaking of the flesh. It is not saying that Jesus looked just like the Father in any physical sense, because God the Father has no physical flesh: He is spirit.

The Word is teaching us that Jesus' life was the image of the Father's life. In every spiritual and mental way Jesus was the express image of the Father. We can look at how Jesus reacted in every situation and know how the Father would have handled that situation. For the first time, in all recorded history, we can come to a proper understanding of God by looking at, not the physical body, but the spiritual and mental life He lived. We can truly come to know Him by knowing the things He did and did not do, and the things He said and did not say.

Another aspect of the person of God is that He is omnipotent: all-powerful. This is also beyond the understanding of finite man. Here again all that we can do is look at Jesus to come to some kind of understanding of the Father, and this mind-boggling attribute.

On one occasion Jesus and His disciples went to a wedding feast. While they were there, the wine gave out. Mary, His mother, was also there. Evidently she was a friend of the family, because she was the one who took the problem to Jesus seeking His help. Setting against a wall were six water pots of stone, after the purification customs of the Jews. He told the servants to fill the pots with water. Then they were to draw from the pots and take to the one in charge of the festivities. When the ruler of the feast drank from the cup, he found the sweetest and best wine he had ever tasted (John 2:1-11). This was quite a demonstration of the omnipotent power of God. It was something that was certainly beyond the finite power of man.

At another time Jesus saw a man who had been born blind. He spat on the ground and made clay, and with the clay anointed the blind man's eyes.

Then He sent him to wash his eyes in the pool of Siloam. When the clay was washed from his eyes, he could see clearly (John 9:1-7). Who else but God could do such a thing, or have the power to do such a thing.

Not only did Jesus heal the blind, but also the lame. He made the deaf to hear and the dumb to speak (Mark 7:37). He cured a withered hand (Mark 3:1-5). He relieved an epileptic of his distressing disease (Matthew 17:14-18). He cast out demons. He cured a woman of an issue of blood (Matthew 9:20-23). And on and on He worked the miracles of God through the omnipotence of God.

Perhaps the greatest display of the omnipotent power of God incarnate was the restoring life to those who had been dead. There are three incidents recorded in the Gospels:

The first took place in the city of Nain. The only son of a widow had died. When Jesus saw the mother weeping He had compassion on her and said, "Weep not." Then He touched the coffin and said, "Young man, I say to you, 'Arise.'" And the dead came to life and began to talk to those standing near (Luke 7:11-15).

The second is recorded in Luke 8:49-56. This is the story of the raising of the daughter of Jairus, the ruler of the synagogue.

The most dramatic of the three is recorded in John 11:1-46. Lazarus, a friend of Jesus had died and been buried four days when Jesus arrived at his tomb. Now some might question the other two incidents, saying that those raised had not been buried and perhaps they were not really dead. But there was no question about Lazarus being dead. By the time Jesus arrived, the body had started to decay:

> Jesus...came to the grave. It was a cave, and a stone lay upon it. Jesus said, "Take away the stone." Martha, the sister of him that was dead, said to him, "Lord, by this time he stinks: for he has been *dead* four days." Jesus said to her, "Said I not to you, that, if you would believe, you should see the glory of God?" Then they took away the stone *from the place* where the dead was laid. And Jesus lifted up *His* eyes, and said, "Father, I thank You that You have heard me. And I know that You always hear me: but because of the people who are standing by I said *it* that they may believe that You have sent me." And when he had spoken this, he cried with a loud voice, "Lazarus, come forth." And he that was dead came forth, bound hand and foot with grave clothes: and his face was bound about with a napkin. Jesus said to them, "Free him, and let him go" (John 11:38-44).

We must come to grips with the fact that God has infinite knowledge, or in simpler terms, God knows all things. It is obvious from Scripture that God can look into the heart or mind of man and read every thought. This is not only so with one man, but with every man. Remember, he knew the hearts of all of those who lived before the Flood: "And God saw that the wickedness of man was great in the earth, and that every imagination of the thoughts of his heart was only evil continually" (Genesis 6:5). So He knows the heart of every man today. It is most difficult for man to fully comprehend the truth that God in His infinite understanding can know the deepest and most secret thoughts of man's mind. This is the trouble Nathanael, one of the twelve, had:

> Philip found Nathanael, and said to him, "We have found him, of whom Moses in the law, and the prophets, wrote, Jesus of Nazareth, the son of Joseph." And Nathanael said to him, "Can there any good thing come out of Nazareth?" Philip said to him, "Come and see." Jesus saw Nathanael coming to Him, and sad of him, "Behold an Israelite indeed, in whom is no deceit!" Nathanael said to him, "How do know me?" Jesus answered and said to him, "Before Philip called you, when you were under the fig tree, I saw you." Nathanael answered and sad to Him, Rabbi, You are the Son of God; You are the King of Israel" (John 1:45-49).

I Chronicles 28:9 testifies that it is a fact whether we believe it or not: "The Lord searches all hearts, and understands all the imaginations of the thoughts." What a sobering fact that is! If we really understood this truth, we would clean the trash out of the closets of our minds and fill them with the wholesome and pure thoughts that a Christian ought to have. Before we think our thoughts, we need to remember that God knows them all.

We also need to know that time creates no problem for God's knowledge. In Psalm 33:13, we read, "The Lord looks from heaven; He sees all of the sons of men." He sees us all. Every man who has ever existed, every man who now exists, and every man who will ever exist is completely known to God. He is able to constantly see all men, past, present, and future. As He sees us now, so He sees our distant ancestors with equal clarity, and so He sees our future offspring. The past, present, and the future are all the same to God.

Man finds God difficult to fully understand because of His infinite presence. Man knows that he cannot be in but one place at a time, and it is difficult to understand that God knows no such limitation. Psalm 139:7-12, expresses this omnipresence of God:

> Where shall I go from Your Spirit? Or where shall I flee from Your presence? If I ascend up into heaven, You *are* there: if I make my bed in hell, behold, You *are there. If* I take the wings of the morning, *and* dwell in the most distant parts of the sea; even there shall Your hand leads me, and Your right hand shall hold me. If I say, 'Surely the darkness shall cover me;' even the night shall be light around me. Yes, the darkness hides nothing from You; but the night shines as the day: the darkness and the light *are* both alike *to You.*

We find the same thought in Jeremiah 23:23-24:

> '*Am* I a God near by,' says the LORD, 'and not a God far away? Can anyone hide himself in secret places that I shall not see him?' says the LORD. 'Do not I fill heaven and earth?' says the LORD.

God in His infinite presence is able to be in all places at all times. Jonah discovered this truth about the Lord God when he tried to run from the command of the Lord. God had told him to go to Nineveh and warn the inhabitants that He was going to destroy them because of their wickedness. Jonah tried to do what many of God's servants have tried to do down through the ages. He would go to some far off place and hide from God. So he took passage on a ship that was to sail for Tarshish (present-day Spain), which was in the opposite direction from Nineveh.

God found Jonah, in the midst of the sea, through a terrible storm. Actually God, in His infinite knowledge, knew where Jonah was all the time. More than that, God was with Jonah all the time. God caused the storm winds to blow to get Jonah's attention, so that Jonah could find himself in relation to the will of God. Sometimes God has to send storms into our lives to get our attention and to show us the way back to Him physically and spiritually.

The ship was on the verge of being destroyed by the storm. Jonah told the captain and crew that he was the cause for the storm and that the only way to handle the situation was to throw him into the sea. In desperation the sailors did as Jonah told them to do, and threw him overboard.

We are told that God prepared a great fish to come and swallow Jonah. For three days and three nights Jonah had space to repent of his sin of running from God. On the third day the great fish coughed Jonah up on shore. Then, in repentance, Jonah could go to Nineveh and be obedient to the command of the Lord (Jonah 1:1-3:4). This makes the truth exceedingly clear: you simply cannot hide from God. In His omniscience and omnipresence He will find you.

God has promised never to leave us nor forsake us:
> Be strong and of have good courage, fear not, nor be afraid of them: for the LORD your God, He is the One who goes with you; he will not fail you, nor forsake you (Deuteronomy 31:6).
>
> Let your life be free of covetousness; and be content with such things as you have: for He has said, "I will never leave you, nor forsake you" (Hebrews 13:5).

Having come to a proper understanding of God, at least as much as the finite mind of man can comprehend the Infinite, we need to come to an understanding of the required and acceptable worship of God.

## -The Proper Worship Of God -

To worship God through mental or material images is sin. This is true because it limits the limitless God, to what can be conceived by the finite mind of man. Mental or physical images simply are man's attempts to squeeze God down into a form small enough to fit into man's finite mind. A mental or material image limits God, because it is saying that the Creator can be likened to the creature. This is exactly what the Lord God said through the prophet Isaiah:
> To whom will you compare Me, and make My equal, and measure me by, that we may be similar? They measure out an abundant amount of gold from their bag, and weigh silver in the balance, and hire a goldsmith; and he makes it into a god: they fall down before it, yes, they worship it. They bear it upon their shoulder, they carry it, and set it in its place, and it stands; from its place it shall not be able to move: indeed, *one* shall cry out to it, yet it cannot answer, nor save him out of his trouble. Remember this, and show yourselves men: bring *it* again to mind, O you transgressors. Remember the former things of old: for I am God, and there is none else; I am God, and there is none like me (Isaiah 46:5-9).

Worshipping God through images, mental or material, limits God, and is sin because it confines Him to a place. Remember God is limitless concerning time and space. This is what God's Word tells us over and over again:
> But will God indeed dwell on the earth? Consider, the heaven and heaven of heavens cannot contain You; how much less this house that I have built (I Kings

8:27).

Thus says the Lord, The heaven *is* My throne, and the earth *is* My footstool: where *is* the house that you build for Me? And where *is* the place of My rest? For all those things My hand has made, and all those things have been, says the Lord (Isaiah 66:1- 2).

However the most High dwells not in temples made with hands; as the prophet said, "Heaven *is* My throne, and earth *is* my footstool: what house will you build for Me?" Says the Lord: "Or what is the place of My rest? Has not My hand made all these things?' (Acts 7:48-50).

It is sin to use images or idols in the worship of God, because it reduces His power to what man can conceive. This was what caused Sarah to laugh when God told Abraham that she would conceive a child, even though she was eighty-nine years old. Sarah's mental image of God was too small to work such a miracle. So the Lord said to Abraham, "Why did Sarah laugh, saying, 'Shall I, who am old, really bear a child?' Is any thing too hard for the LORD?" (Genesis 18:13-14).

It is also sin to use physical or mental images in our worship, because the image becomes the focal point of worship. Soon the mind would fail to remember the all-present, all-knowing, and all-powerful God. The image would be the god.

Even though worship through images may be designed to terminate in God, it is still sin. God said, "You shall not make yourself any graven image, or any likeness of anything that *is* in heaven above, or that *is* in the earth beneath, or that is in the water under the earth: You shall not bow down yourself to them, nor serve them: for I the LORD your God *am* a jealous God" (Exodus 20:4-6). I believe God is saying, "Worship Me as I am, not as you imagine Me to be. Do not limit Me in anyway." We must worship God in spirit and in truth.

In the fourth chapter of the Gospel of John we are told that Jesus left Judea and was returning to Galilee. On the way He stopped outside Sychar, a city of Samaria, and rested at a well, while His disciples had gone into the city to buy food. A Samaritan woman came to the well to draw water, and Jesus asked her for a drink. The old animosities and prejudices between the Jews and the Samaritans reared their ugly heads. She could not believe that a Jew would ask anything from a Samaritan. She did not know Jesus. He was there to win this woman and her village to Himself.

During their conversation the woman made a comment about the worship of God: "Our fathers worshipped on this mountain; and you say, that Jerusalem is the place where men should come to worship" (John 4:20). Jesus' answer to this comment helped the woman find her way back to God, from a sinful life, and it will help us to a better understanding of God and the worship of God:

> Woman, believe me, the hour is coming, when you shall neither in this mountain, nor even at Jerusalem, worship the Father...the hour is coming, and now is that the true worshipers shall worship the Father in spirit and in truth: for the Father seeks such to worship him. God *is* Spirit: and they that worship him must worship Him in spirit and in truth (John 4:21, 23, 24).

It is as Jesus said; if we will worship God then it must be in spirit and in truth. We must worship Him as He really is. The worship must be of spirit to Spirit. For only the spirit of man can really touch or commune with the eternal Spirit from where it came. True spiritual worship is the only worship that allows God to be fully God. It is the only worship that does not limit God.

It is at this point that faith enters into our worship. We must worship by faith. Hebrews 11:6, says, "But without faith it is impossible to please Him: for he who comes to God must believe that He is, and that He rewards those who diligently seek him." God is saying that He wants us to believe that He is, without having to see some image or form. This is at the heart of what Scripture calls faith: "Faith is the confident assurance that what we hope for is going to happen. It becomes the evidence of things we cannot yet see" (Hebrews 11:1). Spiritual worship by faith is actually something that is accomplished by Jesus. He works in our hearts and minds to give us the faith and the desire needed to perform the worship. Without Him working in us we would never be able to worship, as we should.

We must worship God through Jesus, God's Son. For only through the life that Jesus lived, can finite man know the infinite God. Jesus taught exactly this in John 12:45-50:

> He that believes on Me, believes not on Me, but on Him who sent me. And he that sees Me sees Him who sent me. I have come as a light to the world, that whoever believes on Me should not live in darkness. And if any man hears My words, and does not believe, I do not judge him: for I did not came to judge the world, but to save the world. He that rejects Me, and does not receives My words, has One that judges him: the word that I have spoken, the same shall judge him in the last day. For I have not spoken of Myself; but the Father who sent me,

> He gave me a commandment, what I should say, and what I should speak. And I know that His commandment is life everlasting: whatever I speak therefore, even as the Father said to me, so I speak.

Belief in and service to Jesus is the only way we can be acceptable before God. Remember, Jesus said, "No man comes to the Father, but by Me" (John 14:6).

Jesus also said:

> For God did not send His Son into the world to condemn the world, but that the world through Him might be saved. He that believes on Him is not condemned: but he that believes not is condemned already, because he has not believed in the name of the only begotten Son of God (John 3:17-18).

We cannot worship God, unless we are acceptable to Him. We shall never be acceptable to Him if we are making Him less than He is. Have you been making God less than He is, through mental or physical images? If so, then remember, "You shall not make for yourself any carved image" to bow down to in worship.

Have you been worshipping God in spirit and truth, through faith in Jesus? If not, why not give Him proper worship today? He will bless you in your obedience to Him.

# Chapter 4

## Sincere Worship

(Exodus 20:7)
"You shall not use the name of the Lord your God in useless way."

### - Introduction -

Thus far, in our study, we have found three things concerning the Ten Commandments to help us come to a better understanding of God and the worship of God.

In the first chapter, "Law And Grace," we found that the Law is relevant today. It is obvious from Scripture that God expects us to live by His Law. Nowhere in the Bible is it recorded that in becoming a Christian we are freed from obedience to the Law. It does say that we are free from the condemnation of the Law (Romans 8:1-9), but not from obedience. Christ, the incarnate Son of God, said in no uncertain terms that He did not come into this world to destroy the Law. To the contrary He taught us that He came to fulfill the Law, not destroy it. He said that His mission was to fulfill the requirements of the Law. It is stated over and over again that Christ came to satisfy the demands of the Law. The marvelous truth is He came to do for man what man was unable to do for himself.

Therefore man is to live his life in obedience to the Law of God. However this is not to be done in terror of the loss of his life. Any keeping of the Law that man does out of terror is unacceptable to the blessed Giver-Of-The-Law. For man to keep the Law out of terror would make man a mere puppet on a string. To keep the Law out of terror would be the same as being forced or manipulated into doing what God requires. God does not want His creature by force or manipulation. God wants man is to keep the Law out of desire created by love.

Now, it is true that man is to fear God. This fear, however is reverential awe, it is not a fear born out of the wrath of God. Webster say that "awe" is "fear mingled with admiration or reverence; a feeling produced by something majestic, sublime." Then the synonyms are listed as "dread, terror, and horror." Sin makes one stand in "dread" of the wrath of God. Freedom from sin in Christ Jesus makes one stand in "veneration and reverence" of a loving God of Grace.

The questions ring out to all men everywhere, "How can man do less than love the Lord?" And "How can we love God and not be obedient to His Law?" With equal clarity the answers echo back, "Man can do no less than love God." And certainly "All men will render total submission to God's Laws when they kneel before the Righteous Judge in Judgment." We are told that at that time everyone will kneel before Him and confess that He is Christ the Lord. However, such submission and confession is too late for all that have failed to confess Him in this life.

It is also evident that man cannot keep the Law, in and of himself. He simply does not have the wisdom, strength, or courage of will to do so. Life itself shows us the truth of this. Man fell from the grace of God in the beginning because of his inability to keep the Law. Time has not changed this for man. He has been falling and failing ever since. This is the primary reason that Christ came into the world: not to condemn fallen man (see John 3:17), but to save him; not to chastise or criticize man for his failure, but to give him the strength, wisdom, and courage needed to live by God's Law. All this is found to be possible in and through faith in Jesus Christ.

Next, we learned that we must be faithful to God, and worship only Him: "You shall have no other gods before me." God must be our all in all. We must never allow another god to come between the one true God and us. He will have all our love and devotion. He is the only one worthy of such reverence and dedication. God must come first in our lives, and He must have our best.

Then, in chapter three, of our study, we discovered that there is a proper worship of God:

> You shall not make yourself any carved image, or any likeness of anything that *is* in heaven above, or that is in the earth beneath, or that is in the water under the earth: You shall not bow down before them, or serve them: for I the LORD your God am a jealous God, visiting the iniquity of the fathers upon the children to the third and fourth generation of those who hate me; And showing mercy to thousands of those who love me, and keep my commandments (Exodus 20:4-6).

To be able to approach God in acceptable worship, we must first have an accurate understanding of Him. The starting point for gaining a correct understanding of God is that He is Spirit. As Spirit, He is not limited in any way by flesh, time, or space. Therefore we must worship Him in spirit and in truth. We must allow our spirit to touch His Spirit, or the eternal Spirit of God must touch our spirit. Literally He is saying to us, "Worship me as I am, not as you would have Me to be, or imagine Me to be." We must worship Him through faith. It is only with the eye of faith that we can perceive the eternal Spirit. Actually there is no image that we can make of God, who is limitless Spirit.

Now we come to the third Commandment: "You shall not speak the name of the Lord your God in useless way; for the Lord will not judge him guiltless who speaks His name in a useless way" (Exodus 20:7). It is directly related to the first and second Commandments and also to the fourth; for they, like it, all speak of the worship of God. The third Commandment speaks of the Sincere Worship of God.

## - Sincerity In Reverence -

We find two demands in this Law, which must be met in our worship of God. The first of which is a demand for Sincerity in Reverence. God said, "You shall not speak the name of the Lord your God in a useless way" (Exodus 20:7). Yet men can, and do, speak the name of God in a useless way through irreverence. Speaking God's name in a useless way through irreverence is done by treating God's name lightly, or frivolously.

When men act as though the worship of God is unimportant, it is without question treating the name of God frivolously or lightly. It is saying that other things are more important than a time for worship of the one true God. It really matters not if it is mowing the lawn, or playing golf, or going to the mountains, or going to the beach, or if it is simply staying in bed to sleep late on Sunday morning, they all amount to the same thing: treating the name of God lightly or frivolously. At least they do if they come between man and worship of God.

Man can also treat the name of God frivolously or lightly when he acts as though God, Himself, is unimportant. We might consider this the take-it-or-leave-it attitude. It is somewhat like saying, "Oh it is all right to believe in God! Belief in God may have some practical benefits. But it certainly must not be taken to extremes. We would not want to appear too religious or too fanatical." Then that same man will go to a football game or a baseball game or a basketball game, and act as if he has left all his senses at home. He will yell as loudly as he can, and jump up and down in a passionate frenzy in support of his favorite team. He calls that being loyal to his team and being a true fan.

The strange thing is we get the word "fan" from our word "fanatic." Webster's dictionary says that to be a fan means to be "an enthusiastic lover of any sport, such as baseball." But listen to what the same dictionary says about being a fanatic: "One who is intemperately zealous, or wildly extravagant, especially on religious subjects." According to that definition it would appear that it is all right to be "an enthusiastic lover" of sports, but it is "intemperately zealous, or wildly extravagant" if one is serious about God and the worship of God. Not to be completely sold out to God in worship is taking away from the importance of God, and that is treating the name of God in useless way.

Men do the same thing when they treat the service of God as though it is unimportant. There are multitudes of men and women who will give generously of their time in service through various civic and fraternal organizations, who would never get involved in the work of God and His church. It is obvious that they believe the one to be important and the other unimportant. It is a shame, and it is also sin when God is placed on the unimportant side of service. It is treating God's name in useless way.

We also hold the name of God in irreverence when we act as though our life does not depend on Him for our every breath and for everything else that sustains that life. Remember what the Bible tells us about this: "The Lord God formed man of the dust of the ground, and breathed into his nostrils the breath of life; and man became a living soul" (Genesis 2:7).

When the children of Israel were in the wilderness, Moses reminded them saying, "...he humbled you, and allowed you to hunger, and fed you with manna, which you did not know, neither did your fathers know; that he might make you know that man does not live by bread only, but by every word that proceeds out of the mouth of the Lord does man live" (Deuteronomy 8:3). Moses also told Israel, "...he is your life, and the length of your days..." (Deuteronomy 30:20).

Hannah, the mother of Samuel the prophet, in her prayer of thanksgiving said, "The Lord kills, and makes alive: he brings down to the grave, and brings up" (I Samuel 2:6).

The apostle Paul summed it up succinctly, when he said, "God, who made the world and everything in it, since He is Lord of heaven and earth, does not dwell in temples made with hands. Nor is He worshiped with men's hands, as though He needed anything, since He gives to all life, breath, and all things" (Acts 17:24-25) and "For in him we live, and move, and have our being; as certain also of your own poets have said, 'For we are also his offspring'"(Acts 17:28). Therefore not to acknowledge God as the giver and sustainer of life is to treat God's name in useless way through irreverence.

One common way that man treats God's name in a useless way is by using His name in jest, or by making Him the butt of a joke. Such irreverence causes His name to be held up to disrespectful laughter. Paul says that this ought not to be so: "Neither filthiness, nor foolish talking, nor jesting, which are not convenient: but rather giving thanks" (Ephesians 5:4).

It is a dangerous thing to use God's name to take an oath confirming the truth of something when it is false. This is called "stretching the truth" or "telling a white lie" or "playing loose with the truth" by those who do it. The truth of the matter is that it is plain and simple lying. That is exactly what Ananias and Sapphira did, and they died for it (Acts 5:1-10). This is true because it is profaning God's name: "And you shall not swear by my name falsely, neither shall you profane the name of your God: I am the Lord" (Leviticus 19:12). It is treating the name of God in useless way.

The world is full of men who use God's name foolishly, through profanity or cursing. With some people, it seems that every other word is a curse word or some kind of profanity. Instead of their speech being "always with grace, seasoned with salt" (Colossians 4:6) it is peppered with profanity and vulgarity.

It chills my soul to hear the filth that pours from some peoples' mouths; men, women, and even children. It would appear that adults who talk with filthy language are lacking in vocabulary, to say the least. When children, even four, five, and six years old, use vulgar language, it may be they have listened to adults talk this language of the gutter. Parents who set such an example will have much to answer when they face God. Such people also fall into the same classification as those called "profane." Without question, they come under the same condemnation as those who are guilty of false swearing. In the little epistle of James we read a stern admonition against this type of useless treatment of God's name: "Out of the same mouth comes blessing and cursing. My brethren, these things ought not to be so" (James 3:10). James is right; God's name should never be treated in useless. It should never be used irreverently.

Man needs to understand that God's name is holy. Over and over again we are told this in His Word: "Find glory in His holy name: let the heart of those rejoice who seek the LORD" (Psalm 105:3). "He sent redemption to his people: He has guaranteed His covenant will be forever: holy and awe-inspiring is His name." (Psalm 111:9).

Mary, the mother of Christ, in her song of praise to God said, "For He who is mighty has done great things to me; and His name is holy" (Luke 1:49). God's victorious children are pictured in the Revelation as saying, "Who shall not fear You, O Lord, and glorify Your name? For *You* only *are* holy: for all nations will come and worship before You; for Your judgments are shown clearly for all to know" (Revelation 15:4).

Jesus taught His disciples to pray, "Your name is holy" (Luke 11:2). There is no evil in Him. It is impossible for Him to err or commit sin. I have heard it said many times, "God makes no mistakes," and it is true. There are no imperfections in Him. He is flawless perfection. He is the only true standard of right, truth, honor, and justice. Therefore God's name justly deserves sincere reverence.

Giving God's name the reverence due it requires three things. First, it is required that His name be held in the highest esteem. Paul had the right idea when he said concerning Christ Jesus, who was God in human flesh:

> Whereas God also has highly exalted Him, and given Him a name that is above every name: That when the name of Jesus is spoken every knee should bow, and also all things in heaven, all things on earth, and all things under the earth; And that every tongue should confess that Jesus Christ is Lord, to the glory of God the Father (Philippians 2:9-11).

How can we do less than prostrate ourselves at the mention of His holy name? He truly deserves such sincere devotion.

The second thing required of man to give God the reverence due Him is that we take His name seriously. I believe that this is one of the greatest problems we face in our reverence of God. We are perfectly willing to be serious about God when we are in a worship service in the church building. We find no problem with being serious while singing the hymns of praise. It is not too difficult to listen seriously to the sermons, at least if they are lively and interesting; but when we are in our home or on our job, that is another matter. Then we are so busy with other things it is difficult to be seriously concerned about God.

Mostly we try to justify this by saying; "We are just keeping our priorities in line. We will give God His due on His time, but we must keep worship separated from business. They simply don't mix." That may be our defense for relegating God to the back burner of our secular lives, but it is still treating God's name in a useless way.

The prophet Isaiah had no problem with understanding and accepting the seriousness of the Lord's name. When he spoke of the coming of God to earth he said, "His name shall be called Wonderful, Counselor, The mighty God, The everlasting Father, The Prince of Peace" (Isaiah 9:6). It takes only a casual look at the words Isaiah used to see how serious he was about the name of God. If we take a little deeper look into his words we will find ourselves awed by the intensity of his seriousness.

According to the dictionary the word "wonderful" means "something exciting, or strange." That is really too pale a definition of what Isaiah had in mind. It is translated from the Hebrew word "pele'" which means "a miracle, a marvelous thing, or a wonder." When we consider the spaciousness of the full meaning of the word "miracle," as Isaiah uses it, it is obvious that he was awed by the name of God. His mind was trying to express something and someone beyond the reason, or imagination, or ability of natural man to explain.

Counselor is commonly defined as "one who gives advice; especially legal advice." The Hebrew word used by Isaiah is "ya'ats" which means, "to advise, to give counsel, determine, devise, guide, purpose." To advise or give counsel speaks of wisdom or knowledge. In this instance Isaiah is speaking of the infinitely wise God. He is the only one capable of knowing the past, present, and future. He is the only one who can know all the possibilities in every situation. Therefore He is the true Counselor, because His advice will always be perfect. He is also the perfect Counselor because His guidance will never cause one to take a faulty step, nor will He cause a wrong direction to be taken. Because He is the Righteous Judge of heaven and earth, the Supreme Counselor, it is in His right to determine the outcome and consequences of all circumstances of life. As the Unerring Architect, of all created things, His counsel is to be obeyed without question. Because He knows the end from the beginning, He has the perfect right to devise and propose for His creation, as He desires.

Isaiah's term "the Mighty God" is extremely interesting in the Hebrew language. The word for "Mighty" is "gibbowr" which means "powerful or mighty." The word for "God" is "'el," which also means "the Almighty God." Together we have "The Powerful Almighty God." Such usage can only mean that He is the God of unlimited or infinite power. There is certainly none other like Him, nor will there ever be.

"Everlasting Father" in the Hebrew is "'ad 'ab." The "'ad" can be translated "Eternal," but when it is done so it must be in the sense of "perpetuity or perpetually." Therefore it means "Eternally self-existent" or "without beginning or ending." The "'ab" means, "Father in a literal and figurative sense, and also in an immediate and remote sense." This can, most surely, be interpreted "Omniscient Father of the physical and spiritual." When we take the two words together, we get "Omniscient Father of the physical and spiritual who has no beginning nor ending." Here is a picture of the Eternally Self-Existent Omnipresent Father God. His presence is unlimited. No matter where we may go He is still our Father. He has always been with us, and He will always be with us. He is our Father physically because He is our Creator. Spiritually He is our Father, because He is our Redeemer. He will be our Father when all other fathers are gone. He will be our Father when all other fathers fail.

Prince of Peace, Hebrew "Sar Shalowm," is certainly as fitting, if not more fitting, than all the other names Isaiah uses to name the Great God who was to come to earth and inhabit human flesh.

"Sar" means "Head person, Captain, Chief, Governor, Keeper, Lord,

Master, Prince." All these titles have been applied to Jesus: In Joshua 5:13-15, He is called the Captain of the Lord's Host. In Hebrews 2:10, He is called the Captain of Salvation. In Ephesians 2:20, and in I Peter 2:6; He is called the Chief Cornerstone. In I Peter 5:4, He is called the Chief Shepherd. He is called the Governor in Isaiah 9:6-7, and Matthew 2:6. In Psalm 121:5, it is said, "The Lord is your Keeper."

All the way through the Bible God is called the Lord. In Exodus 3:14-15, God calls Himself by the term Lord: It says in verse 14, "And God said to Moses, 'I AM WHO I AM:' and He said, 'Thus shall you say to the children of Israel, "I AM has sent me to you."'" Then, in verse 15, He explains that this is the meaning of "LORD:" "And God also said to Moses, 'Thus shall you say to the children of Israel, "The LORD God of your fathers, the God of Abraham, the God of Isaac, and the God of Jacob, has sent me to you: this *is* My name forever, and by this I will be remembered by all generations."

Over and over again Jesus called Himself "I AM": "I Am the way, I Am the truth, I Am the life, I Am the vine" John 14:6; 15:1. In Acts 4:11 and I Peter 2:7, He is called the "Head of the corner." In I Corinthians 11:3, Paul says He is the "Head of every man." In Ephesians 1:22, Paul tells us that God made Him "Head over all things." According to Ephesians 5:23, He is "Head of the church." Jesus said that He was the "Master" in Matthew 23:10 and John 13:13. In Ephesians 6:9 and Colossians 4:1, Paul tells us that Christ is our "Master in heaven." In Acts 3:15; Peter calls Him the Prince of life. Peter also said in Acts 5:31, "God has exalted Him to His right hand to be Prince and Savior, and by Him to give repentance to Israel, and forgiveness of sins."

"Shalowm" means "safe, well, happy, prosperous, peace." So, if we put "Sar" with "Shalowm" we come up with "Head Person, Captain, Chief, Governor, Keeper, LORD, Master, and Prince of safety, health, happiness, prosperity, and peace." Now, that is a name that can really be taken seriously. It is truly as the Apostle Paul said "Christ *is* all and in all."

The third thing required of us in giving proper reverence to the Name of God is that it must be used wisely. After the foregoing consideration of the meaning of the names given to God by Isaiah, I really think that it would be redundant to dwell further on the names of God, except for one more verse of Scripture: "And He has written on His garment, and on His thigh a name King of kings, and Lord of lords" (Revelation 19:16). Such appellations demand that we be extremely discreet in the use of such a holy, powerful, blessed name. If we put all these names together, it becomes apparent that His name is truly to be honored in Reverential Sincerity.

## - Sincerity In Life -

This brings us the second demand that we find in this Commandment: For sincerity in Life. God said, "You shall not speak the name of the Lord your God in a useless way." Yet men do treat God's name in useless way, through inconsistent living. Unfortunately this is true of Christians. There are multitudes of Christian people who do not live according to God's will for their lives. They are members of the church, but they attend church infrequently, or never. Generally, when they are in church, it is on special occasions: Christmas, Easter, or when the children are performing, or there is a special supper.

They may hold a job in the church, but don't expect them to be faithful in the performance of that job. They give into the offering of the church, when they are there, though it is not too likely that they will tithe. It may be possible to see them in Prayer Service on Wednesday night, but don't hold your breath waiting for them to appear. You might as well expect to see it snow in July as to see them in a business meeting. They do little talking about their relationship to the Lord and His church. Perhaps this is true because their relationship with Him is so stunted in growth. They will almost never speak to a lost soul about the need of Christ and salvation. It would seem that they are ashamed of their Lord and His salvation. They are so consumed with making a living and getting ahead in life and enjoying all that God has blessed them with that they really have no time for God. Making money is more important than Christian ethics, so their business practices are questionable if not dishonest. They will ignore the truth to accomplish an end. They will swear to a lie if it will further their business. They say they belong to God, but their lives fail to show it. All this, or any part of this, adds up to taking the name of God in vain.

Then there are those professors of Christ: The ones who say they know God, but who have never really given God their lives. They may do all the things expected of a Christian: Regular attendance in all church services, even business meetings. They may hold several positions in the work of the church. Most likely they will give systematically to the offerings of the church; they may even tithe. You probably won't have to listen extremely closely to be able to hear these ones braying about all they do for God and the church. Their whole professions are built on their goodness and on what they have done and what they are doing for the Lord. These types of church members will spread the good news about their greatness far and wide.

Such people can always tell you what is wrong with the church, its plans, people, and pastor. It is almost impossible for people like this to be satisfied with what is going on in the Lord's work through the local church, or through the mission programs. The problem is they are living a lie, first and last. Their name is Judas. They are like those of whom the Lord spoke in Matthew 7:21-23:

> Not every one who says to Me, 'Lord, Lord,' will enter into the kingdom of heaven; but he who does the will of my Father who is in heaven. Many will say to Me in that day, 'Lord, Lord, have we not prophesied in Your name? And in Your name we have cast out devils? And in Your name we have done many wonderful works?' And then will I answer them, 'I never knew you: depart from me, you who do the works of iniquity.'

For all their loud profession of being God's children, they were never saved, because He never knew them.

This is also true of the blatantly lost. They are perfectly honest in their relationship to the Lord: they have none! This is their problem. They were created in the image of God, yet they do not live for God. In fact they have rejected God and His will for their lives completely. They want nothing to do with Him. They want Him to leave them alone. They want to be their own god. They want to make all the choices and decisions. They believe they are capable of living good enough that they should be acceptable of man and God. They owe God for their existence, but they will not acknowledge it. They too are living a lie. They too are treating God's name in a useless way, by their refusal to honor Him as God and Savior.

God says He "will not judge him guiltless who treats His name in a useless way." This is a fearful statement if it is clearly heard. In simple terms it means that the man who treats God's name in useless way will be called into account. They will stand in the Judgment. The lost will hear the words, "Depart from me, you who are cursed, into everlasting fire, prepared for the devil and his angels" (Matthew 25:41). The Christian will hear his Lord say, "I gave you so little to be faithful in, could you not have been more faithful than you have?" Oh, he will be saved from the sentence passed down on the lost, but due only to what Christ did. Paul speaks so well to this:

> For we are laborers together with God: you are God's field, *you are* God's building. According to the grace of God, which is given to me, as a wise master builder, I have laid the foundation, and another builds on it. But let every man take heed how he builds on it. For no other foundation can any man lay than that which is

laid, which is Jesus Christ. Now if any man builds on this foundation out of gold, silver, precious stones, wood, hay, stubble; Every man's work shall be clearly seen for what it is: for the day shall declare it, because it shall be revealed by a test of fire; and that fire will try every man's work of what sort it is. If any man's work, which he has built thereon, stands the test of fire, he shall receive a reward. If any man's work shall be burned, he will suffer loss: but he himself shall be saved; yet so as by fire (I Corinthians 3:9-15).

The saved will have to answer for their lack of commitment in this life, because Christ has answered for their life to come. They are saved now, and will be saved in Heaven. But, believe me, Hell fire can burn and sear in this life as well as in the life to come.

If one is a professing Christian and does not suffer in this life for his inconsistent living, it is because he is not a Christian and never was. He will suffer in the torments of Hell to come.

The lost, professor or not, will be found guilty and condemned. Trying to live a Christian life when you are not a Christian is still a lie, and it is treating God's name in useless way.

# Chapter 5

## A Day Of Worship

(Exodus 20:8-11)
"Remember the Sabbath day, to keep it holy. Six days you shall labor, and do all your work: But the seventh day *is* the Sabbath of the LORD your God: in it you shall not do any work, you, your son, or your daughter, your manservant, or your maidservant, your cattle, or the stranger who *is* within your gates: For *in* six days the LORD made heaven and earth, the sea, and all that *is* in them, and rested the seventh day: therefore the LORD blessed the Sabbath day, and hallowed it."

### - Introduction -

In the last chapter, we said that there is a direct relationship between the first four Commandments. It is true that there is a connection in that the first four Commandments are all dealing with man's relationship to God: they are God-ward in direction. However, there is another connection that we need to consider. They all four deal with man's worship of God.

In the first Commandment we are commanded to worship the Lord God, and none other: "You shall have no other gods before Me" (Exodus 20:3). God will have our complete attention. He will not share our worship with anyone or anything. To give less than absolute fidelity to God is idolatry. It is idolatry because there is something else that is being revered beside the Lord. To worship anything else, even if God is being included in your worship is idolatry, and idolatry is sin.

In the Second Commandment we are instructed to worship God directly:

> You shall not make for yourself any carved image, or any likeness of anything that *is* in heaven above, or that *is* in the earth beneath, or that *is* in the water under the earth: You shall not bow down yourself to them, or serve them: for I the Lord your God am a jealous God, visiting the iniquity of the fathers upon the children to the third and fourth generation of those who hate Me;

And showing mercy to thousands of those who love Me,
and keep My commandments (Exodus 20:4-6).

Not only is God a jealous God, who will not tolerate our worship of other gods, but also He will not allow our worship of Him to be directed through any type of image or statue or picture. We must remember that God is Spirit, and our worship of Him must be in spirit and in truth (see John 4:23). He wants us to let Him be who He is and all that He is. He does not want us to limit Him in any way.

The third thing we learned is that we are commanded to worship God in sincerity: "You shall not use the name of the Lord your God in useless way; for the Lord will not judge him guiltless who uses His name in a useless way" (Exodus 20:7). There must be no useless or irreverent use of God's name. There must be no irreverence of any kind, whether in life, or in service, or in speech.

This brings us to the Fourth Commandment: "Remember the Sabbath day, to keep it holy" (Exodus 20:8). In this Commandment we find seven things that we must deal with concerning special days of worship.

## -The Integrity Of Labor -

First, we are commanded by the Lord God: "Six days shall you labor, and do all your work..." (Exodus 20:9). Here the emphasis is on man's responsibility to work. In plain words we are told that work is in the will of God for man.

There is a terrible misconception that needs to be cleared from the mind of many people concerning work. There are some who would teach that work came because of sin. They would point to what God said to Adam after the fall:
> Because you have listened to the voice of your wife, and have eaten of the tree, which I commanded you, saying, 'You shall not eat of it:' the ground is cursed for your sake. It will produce thorns and thistles to make your labor difficult to grow the grain you will eat: for now you will eat bread that is produced by the sweat of your face, until you return to the ground. For you were made out of the dust of the earth: for dust you are, and to dust you will return (Genesis 3:17-19),

Then they would say, "That plainly states that labor came because of sin." Let us examine these verses and see if they teach such a doctrine.

It says, "The ground is cursed for your sake." Then it states the curse put on the ground: It will produce thorns and thistles. There will be no labor required for the land to produce weeds. From the fall of man onward these things will grow as a hindrance to man's labor. From the fall of man onward man will have to labor under difficult conditions. Now his work will be so difficult that he will be drenched in sweat; it will run down his forehead and into his eyes, and make him miserable. Now his labor will be so difficult that his muscles will ache with fatigue. Now his hands will become blistered and raw from the hard labor that will be his to perform. Now there will be no reaching up into the nearest tree to satisfy of his hunger. Now it will require backbreaking cultivation and care for those trees to produce the fruit to fill the empty stomach. We could continue, but this should be sufficient to show that this says nothing about man being cursed with labor because of sin. This simply says that man's labor is made rigorous due to sin.

A little closer look at the Word and we will see that labor, or work, preceded sin. When we look at the story of the creation we see God working. It says, "In the beginning God created the heaven and the earth" (Genesis 1:1), and "...God made the firmament, and divided the waters" (Genesis 1:7), and "...God made two great lights" (Genesis 1:16), and "...God created...every living creature" (Genesis 1:21), and "...God said, 'Let us make man in our image, after our likeness'" (Genesis 1:26). Now His "creative acts" were work, just as "building or making" something is work. Genesis 2:2, says, "And on the seventh day God ended his work which he had made; and he rested on the seventh day from all his work which he had completed." That plainly says that God worked in creating all things. Now, God cannot sin; or so the Bible tells us over and over again. That being so, and it is, then because God "labored" or "worked" is absolute proof that "work" is not sin, nor is it the product of sin.

Now note another positive concerning labor. After each act of creation God saw that, "It was good" (Genesis 1:4, 10, 12, 18, 21, and 25), until He created man, and then it is recorded, "And God saw everything that He had made, and, behold, it was very good..." (Genesis 1:31). Since God's work is "good" and "very good," it cannot be related to sin in any way. Also note that God considered His work so "very good," that He set a memorial day to commemorate it (Genesis 2:2).

Now let us seek in the Word when labor was given to man and determine if it came before or after his fall into sin. Go back to the first chapter of Genesis and there in the twenty-eighth verse, following man's creation, God said to Adam and Eve, "Be fruitful, and multiply, and replenish the earth, and subdue it: and have dominion over every living thing that moves on the earth." The words "subdue" and "have dominion," indicate that labor would be involved. In Genesis 2:8-15, we are told "God planted a garden eastward in Eden; and there he put the man whom he had formed" (v.8).

Then we are told why He placed the man in the garden: "to dress it and to keep it" (v. 15). To dress and keep a garden requires labor of some kind. So here we find the beginning of labor, and it was before man had sinned. Therefore labor did not come into the world as a result of sin, nor was it placed on man as a curse because he had sinned.

God gave man labor as a gift, and He gave it to man not only because it was good but also for man's good. The first evidence that God gave labor to man for man's good is manifest because it is a blessing. On the surface this may seem to be a foolish idea, but with a little thought one can see that it is true. The blessing of God on the one who works or labors can be seen in that God instructed man to work: "Be fruitful, and multiply, and replenish the earth, and subdue it: and have dominion over the fish of the sea, and over the fowl of the air, and over every living thing that moves on the earth" (Genesis 1:28). Now, if God instructs man to do something, then it follows that the thing given will surely bless man's life. God never tells man to do anything that is wrong or harmful to him. Not only did God instruct man to work, but also He then gave man a place to do his work: "...the Lord God planted a garden eastward in Eden; and there he put the man whom he had formed... to dress it and to keep it" (Genesis 2:8, 15). As God gives only good instructions to His creation, He also gives only good gifts. Therefore the gift of a place to work is a blessing just as work is good.

This Fourth Commandment is a direct command for man to work: "Six days you shall labor, and do all your work..." (Exodus 20:9). This command is repeated in Exodus 23:12, "Six days you shall do your work..." and Exodus 34:21, "Six days you shall work..." and again in Leviticus 23:3, "Six days shall work be done..." Moses went on and emphasized this command in his final book, "Six days you shall labor, and do all your work" (Deuteronomy 5:13). A ruler of the synagogue quoted this command to Jesus, "There are six days in which men ought to work" (Luke 13:14). It is true that this religious leader used this command for the wrong motive, but the fact remains that it is true that God intends for man to work. Paul taught this truth when he said to the elders of the church in Ephesus, "I have showed you all things, how that so laboring you ought to support the weak..." (Acts 20:35). Paul also wrote to the church at Ephesus these words, "Let him that stole steal no more: but rather let him labor, working with his hands the thing which is good, that he may have to give to him who has a need" (Ephesians 4:28). There is no plainer teaching in Scripture than that God wants man to work. Now if God teaches man that he is to labor for his living then it comes as a blessing from God; therefore, it is for man's good.

It is also commanded by God that the one who labors must be compensated for his labor. "The wages of him who is hired shall not remain with you all night until the morning" (Leviticus 19:13). The same idea is taught in Deuteronomy 25:4, "You shall not muzzle the ox when he treads out the corn." Concerning that verse Paul says, "Does God take care for oxen? Or did He say this altogether for our sakes? For our sakes, no doubt, this is written: that he that plows should plow in hope; and that he who threshes in hope should be partaker of his hope" (I Corinthians 9:9-10). Likewise labor was given as a means for man to earn a living, and so it becomes a blessing to man. When you add to that blessing the blessing of God on man to have the physical strength with which he labors in earning his living, then we find the good multiplied.

Labor is also good in that it is honorable. The Psalmist has something most pointed to say here: "For you shall eat the labor of your hands: happy shall you be, and it shall be well with you" (Psalm 128:2). Such a statement can only be made about the honorable man. Actually, concerning the virtue of labor, need we go any further than to say that God labored and so did Jesus, the blessed Son of God. Jesus labored in the creation, and we know that He also labored in His humanity: He was a carpenter, following in the footsteps of His stepfather Joseph. In Jesus' day carpentry was hard labor. There is little doubt that Jesus left the carpenter shop at the end of the day with aching hands, arms, shoulders, back, and legs. Now if God labored, and Jesus labored (in glory and in humanity), then labor is honorable. It is certainly a fact that God, Father, Son, and Spirit, can do nothing, and would do nothing dishonorable.

Also with that kind of labor, the physically tiring labor that Jesus did as a carpenter, comes another blessing: the sweet sleep of the one who laborers in honest work. "The sleep of a laboring man is sweet, whether he eat little or much" (Ecclesiastes 5:12). The Wise Man was saying, "It really does not matter how much you earn by your labor. Honorable labor brings a clear conscience that sleeps sweetly at bedtime."

Labor, as we have said, is necessary because it is commanded for man by God. It is also necessary in that through it we serve and honor God. If there were no other reasons for labor being good, these would make it good and honorable; these would make it a blessing both to man and to God.

The fact that God commands man to work makes being lazy a sin and the lazy person a sinner. The writer of Proverbs says, "The way of the lazy man is like a hedge of thorns" (Proverbs 15:19). In other words his progress is hindered. He is barred from success. In the same book we hear that the lazy person will be impoverished (Proverbs 6:6-11; 24:30-34). Our Lord taught this idea in Luke 19:12-27. The one-talent man was certainly lazy, and he was most assuredly impoverished. Jesus classified the man with one talent as being His enemy (see verse 27). There is no way to be more impoverished than to not have Jesus as Savior and Lord.

The current practice of our time is surely contrary to God and His Word in this matter. Many men today say, "Let us give the man who will not work a guaranteed income." Paul, speaking for the Lord, under His inspiration said, "If anyone will not work, neither shall he eat" (II Thessalonians 3:10). Certainly this has nothing to do with the man who cannot work due to physical or mental inability; he must be cared for because he cannot care for himself. God teaches us to care for the needy. But the lazy man is not needy; he is worthless and good for nothing. We need to lead such a man to a saving knowledge of Jesus Christ, which will cure him of being lazy and make of him a useful citizen.

## - Time For A Day Of Rest -

This Commandment teaches man to set aside one day in seven for rest from his labor: "But the seventh day...you shall not do any work...For in six days the Lord made Heaven and earth, the sea, and all that is in them, and rested the seventh day" (Exodus 20:10-11). After six days of labor man needs a day of rest. God in His wisdom knew that if man was to be at his best, he must rest his body one day out of seven. This is true for the sake of a long life of labor for self and family. And it is also true for a long life of service for God.

How quickly the body will wear out if it is not rested periodically. The psychologists of our time have made extensive studies of man's need for rest, and have discovered that man is much more productive when he has proper times of rest. Large companies are extending the break-times and providing restful activities for their employees to take advantage of the improved productivity that they have been told would be the result. But God knew this from the beginning therefore He commanded man to take a day of rest from his labors. Isn't it amazing how much we can learn from God's Word concerning everyday affairs? Reading God's Word is so enlightening, and it is certainly a lot less expensive than hiring psychologists to do studies for us.

God commanded man to take this day of rest because He knew that man, in and of himself, would not take such a day. Man is so greedy and selfish that he will work all seven days of the week without regard to his physical needs. He wants more and more of the good things of life, so he will destroy himself to get them.

## - Time For A Day Of Worship -

This commandment was given because after six days for self, man needs a day for God:

> "Remember the Sabbath day, to keep it holy. Six days you shall labor, and do all your work: But the seventh day *is* the Sabbath of the LORD your God: in it you shall not do any work, you, your son, or your daughter, your manservant, or your maidservant, your cattle, or the stranger who *is* within your gates: For *in* six days the LORD made heaven and earth, the sea, and all that is in them, and rested the seventh day: therefore the LORD blessed the Sabbath day, and hallowed it" (Exodus 20:8-11).

To understand this need we must consider the meaning of the word "Sabbath," as used here. The word is a transliteration of the Hebrew word "shabbath," the intensive form of the root word "sheath." The root word means "to repose, to cease exertion, to celebrate, to rest." Therefore the word "shabbath," carries these meanings with more force implied. We have already considered the meaning of a day of physical rest. Now the word must be considered in its context to be speaking of "a day set aside for God: "Remember the Sabbath day to keep it holy...the Lord blessed the Sabbath day, and hallowed it." Man needs a day in which to honor God's will for his life, a day for expressing his love for God, and a day for God's holy things.

God did not intend for this "Day for Holy things" to be optional for man. God appointed the day, and commanded man to observe it. Actually God appointed this "holy time" by example as well as by precept or command: Remember, if the Lord rested from His labor, so must man.

A day of worship of the One True God is as necessary for man as is a day of physical rest. As one can become bone weary from labor, so also the soul can become weary and in need of rest. Worship satisfies the need of the soul for rest that cannot be satisfied in any other way. Jesus expressed this truth in Matthew 11:28-30:

> Come to me, all *you* who labor and carry a heavy burden, and I will give you rest. Take my yoke on you, and learn from me; for I am meek and lowly in heart: and you will find rest for your souls. For my yoke *is* easy, and my burden is light

The early disciples also recognized this truth for we are told that "they continued faithfully in the apostles' doctrine and fellowship, and in breaking of bread, and in prayers" (Acts 2:42), and "And let us consider one another to stir up love and good works: Not forsaking the assembling of ourselves together, as the practice of some *is*; but encouraging one another:

and even more so, as you see the day of His return approaching." (Hebrews 10:24-25). They understood that a time apart from the world was necessary for God's children if they were to be strengthened for life in a pagan world. It is that time of sharing among God's people that provides that strength. After six days for the affairs of self, man needs a day for the concerns of God: A day to remember Him as Creator; a day to remember Him as provider; a day to remember Him as Redeemer; a day to praise, and worship Him.

Six days in this sin plagued world makes a day of drawing away to the higher plane of worship indispensable. God has commanded us to separate ourselves from the world in communion with Him. We need the time to renew our closeness to God, to receive spiritual nourishment and to receive spiritual power.

In the wilderness temptation, Jesus quoted from Deuteronomy 8:3, in answer to Satan, "It is written, 'Man shall not live by bread alone, but by every word that come from the mouth of God.'" (Matthew 4:4). Jesus knew the value of a daily study of God's Word to face temptation when it comes. He also knew that on the Sabbath we need to enter God's house and abide with God's people for the best of God's table blessings: "And He came to Nazareth, where He had been brought up: and, as He was accustomed to doing, He went to the synagogue on the Sabbath day, and stood up to read" (Luke 4:16). It should be noted here that Jesus was accustomed to worshiping God in God's house on God's Day, but He also took part in the service: He "read" from the Word of God. It is in God's House, with His people, and in full participation, that the soul is fed to its fullest. It is in the feeding of the soul that we are prepared to serve God and witness for God.

## - Time For A Day Of Commemoration -

The Sabbath was also given as a memorial to creation:
> "Therefore the heavens and the earth were finished, and all the multitude of them. And on the seventh day God finished His work, which He had done; and He rested on the seventh day from all His work, which he had done. And God blessed the seventh day, and sanctified it: because that in it He had rested from all His work, which God created and made" (Exodus 20:11).

We are to remember how God gave us our most beautiful earthly home, and all the blessings that pertain to it and its universe.

The Sabbath Day was to commemorate God's deliverance of the Hebrew people from bondage. God said to them in Exodus 20:2, "I am the

LORD your God, who brought you out of the land of Egypt, out of the house of bondage." Therefore He commanded them to "Remember the Sabbath day, to keep it holy" (Exodus 20:8). They had served in hard bondage in Egypt, now they were free.

So, also the first day of the week commemorates our freedom, as Christians, from sin through Jesus Christ: our eternal deliverance from the chains and bondage of sin and death:

> "Now when *Jesus* was raised early the first *day* of the week..." (Mark 16:9) and "And on the first *day* of the week, when the disciples came together to break bread..." (Acts 20:7) and "On the first *day* of the week let every one of you lay by him in store, as *God* has prospered him, that there be no gatherings when I come." (I Corinthians 16:2).

For the Jews coming out of Egypt, the Sabbath day was kept in anticipation of the coming rest in the Promised Land. This must have been a blessing for them during the forty years of wandering. Each Sabbath they were reminded that one day there would be a permanent rest for them in Canaan. Likewise, the Christian should be in constant anticipation of our rest in God's Eternal Kingdom, that eternal Promised Land. Each Lord's Day should intensify that anticipation.

## - The Seventh Day -

When God speaks of the seventh day, what does He mean? Saturday was and still is the Jewish Sabbath. Jews have held tenaciously to the seventh day as being the correct day of worship. We also have Christian denominations that hold to Saturday as the proper day to worship God in Christ.

The determination of these groups to hold to this practice flies in the face of the prophecy written in Hosea 2:11. There God say, "I will also cause all her mirth to cease, her feast days, her new moons, and her sabbaths, and all her solemn feasts." The fulfillment of this prophecy is found in part during the Assyrian captivity, but the ultimate fulfillment is by Christ on the cross and in His resurrection. This is alluded to by the Apostle Paul in Colossians 2:13-15:

> And you, being dead in your sins and the uncircumcision of your flesh, He has quickened together with Him, having forgiven you all trespasses; Blotting out the handwriting of ordinances that was against us, which was contrary to us, and took it out of the way, nailing it

to His cross; *And* having spoiled principalities and powers, He made a show of them openly, triumphing over them in it.

Christ nailed the Law to the cross so that we would not have to answer to it any longer. He arose on the first day of the week, Sunday, setting it as the New Covenant Sabbath. This is verified by when the early church met to worship, and I repeat the references for conveniences sake:

> "Now when *Jesus* was raised early the first *day* of the week..." (Mark 16:9) and "And on the first *day* of the week, when the disciples came together to break bread..." (Acts 20:7) and "On the first *day* of the week let every one of you lay by him in store, as *God* has prospered him, that there be no gatherings when I come." (I Corinthians 16:2).

I can understand the Jews ignoring Hosea's prophecy and certainly anything written in the New Testament. They do not believe in Christ or the New Testament. I have, however, a problem with Christians ignoring what is the basis of all that gives them reason for existence. Christ and the New Testament are the foundation of all faith and practice for the Christian.

God has given the Christian the Lord's Day, or the First Day of the Week as our day of worship. As the seventh day commemorates the creation of the world, the First Day commemorates the redemption of the world through Jesus Christ. Actually, the Christian Sabbath is a memorial to the New Creation of the saved in the Lord Jesus. It is also a memorial to the creation of a New World that shall be ours when our Lord comes to wind up the affairs of this old world. We have our Lord's promise in this matter:

> In my Father's house are many mansions: I would have told you if this was not true. I go to prepare a place for you. And if I go and prepare a place for you, I will come again, and receive you to Myself; that where I am, you may be also (John 14:2-3).

The apostle John was privileged to see a vision of that New World. You can read about what John saw in Revelation chapters 21 and 22.

## - The Keeping Of The Special Day -

"...you shall not work on this day..." (Exodus 20:10). Just what is involved in this prohibition? Moses, in interpreting the Law, said:

> Six days shall work be done, but on the seventh day there shall be to you a holy day, a Sabbath of rest to the Lord: whoever does work therein shall be put to

death. You shall kindle no fire throughout your habitations on the Sabbath day (Exodus 35:2-3).

The Jews went so far in their prohibiting labor of any kind on the Sabbath that it was almost impossible to do anything at all. This strict adherence to the Law can be understood in the light of Moses' interpretation of this commandment. In Acts 1:12, one prohibition of the Jews is mentioned: "Then they returned to Jerusalem from the mount of Olives, which is a Sabbath day's journey from Jerusalem." The distance mentioned in the verse is about one half a mile. This was the distance that could be traveled on a Sabbath day and still stay within the limits of this Law, as the Jews interpreted it.

I once heard of a Jewish family that was so orthodox that one bitter winter they failed to light the heaters in their home before 6:00 p.m. on Friday, so they did without heat until 6:00 p.m. on Saturday. They also nearly froze to death. Were, and are, such stringent measures necessary? Does God really expect such explicit observance of this Commandment?

For many years I was taught that this commandment applied to the Christian in the following ways:

1) It prohibited labor for selfish reasons. If the labor is performed purely for the sake of profit then such labor was a breach of this Law and therefore it was sin.
2) It prohibited labor that interferes with worship. If the labor was performed during the hours of worship conducted by our church -- Sunday from 9:45 a.m. to 12:00 Noon, and from 6:00 p.m. to 8:00 p.m.; Wednesday from 7:30 p.m. to 8:30 p.m.; Revival times, etc. -- then it was wrong. Such times were sacred, because they were the only times that God could be worshipped. Everybody knew that any labor done during those hours shattered this Law and was a grievous sin.
3) It prohibited patronizing businesses that ignore the Lord's Day. To trade with any such business, either to buy or sell, was a serious violation of this Law. Such conduct would be giving direct support to the business in their sin, and would make us partners with them in their sin.
4) It permitted labor that shows mercy such as feeding and care of animals. A favorite saying was, "If the ox is in the ditch, we must get it out." It always amazed me how much territory the word "ox" covered. The Bible was speaking of the humane care of dumb beasts, but

man had extended it to include any pressing situation that needed to be corrected. Also included in labor that shows mercy would be labor that helps our fellow man.
In this category would be included doctors, nurses, pharmacists, and the witnesses of salvation.

Now all the above were constricted or expanded according to individual minds or ideas. Such constriction or expansion of laws or rules is generally practiced by all people to suit their own life style. Elihu, in the Book of Job, has this to say about such practice, "Should it be according to your mind?" In other words, Elihu was saying, "If God's Law can be interpreted to fit your ideas and desires then why not by my ideas and desires?" I think the question is "Can any human interpretation of God's Word be trusted absolutely?" I do not think so.

However, after much study and deliberation, I have reached a far different opinion about how this commandment applies to the New Testament dispensation. As a religious practice it does not force on us a responsibility, so much as it extends to us a great blessing. The real question we must ask, in relation to the possibility of shattering some religious taboo is not, "Shall I by doing such and such a deed break God's Law," but instead "Shall I by doing the deed miss being blessed by God?" If we ever really get hold of the true meaning of the day, then all things concerning it will fall into their rightful place and all questions that may be asked concerning it will be properly answered.

We need to see that it is a day of celebration and victory. It is certainly not a day of slavery, but a day of freedom. There is no place in it for doom, or gloom but only delight. It is a day in which we can say to the world, we are more than some profession or title or business or job; we are the eternal children of God, redeemed by Jesus Christ, His blessed Son. It is a day in which we can show the world that we are its lords and masters, and not the other way around. It is a day when we proclaim that our real citizenship is in the eternal kingdom of our heavenly Father.

One Sabbath, Jesus and His disciples passed through a grain field. His disciples being hungry began to gather heads of wheat. They rolled the kernels between their palms to separate the chaff from the grain, and began to eat the grain. As was always the case, the super pious Pharisees were there to pronounce judgment on Jesus and His followers for desecrating the Sabbath. When people get to nit picking, there is no limit to which they will go with their quibbling and faultfinding. In answer Jesus simply said that what His disciples did was really no different from what King David did when he and his men were hungry, and went into the house of God and ate the consecrated bread that was on the altar. Then He made a penetrating statement that we need to consider: "The Sabbath was made for man, and not man for the Sabbath: Therefore the Son of man is Lord also of the Sabbath" (Mark 2:23-28).

The Son of man is Lord of all men, and of all things that pertain to men, even the Sabbath. Christ is the Lord of love. He is also the Lord of the Law. If He by example or decree interprets the law in a way that is different from our interpretation, be certain that it is within His prerogative to do so. He alone is the only one who can rightly interpret His Law. Also know that whatever He does is done for love's sake. In any case it is pure nonsense to put the means before the end. If the Sabbath was given to help man then how foolish to allow it to hurt man by taking the joy out of the day!

## - Those Who Are To Keep The Day -

"Six days you shall labor, and do all your work: But the seventh day *is* the Sabbath of the LORD your God: in it you shall not do any work, you, your son, or your daughter, your manservant, or your maidservant, your cattle, or the stranger who *is* within your gates" (Exodus 20:10). This is a most inclusive list of those who are to keep the Sabbath. There are seven classifications of persons in the list, and we shall deal with each one individually.

Of whom was God speaking when He said, "you?" Considering the time in which He spoke these words, and the context as a whole, we must conclude that He was speaking to the men, the heads of households, the husbands, fathers, and providers. He, who was made in the image of God, has the greatest responsibility in this matter. But we must understand that He was also speaking to the women of the households, the wives, the mothers, and the caretakers of the home. In no way are women being ignored by not being specifically mentioned. It is as God said, "They shall be one flesh" (Genesis 2:24). If that is true, then it is impossible to speak of one without including the other. The "you" of this verse is "man and wife."

Then God speaks of the children: "sons and daughters." The responsibility for their religious education falls on the parents. Remember, we teach by example as well as by precept. The old saying is true, "We must take our children to church, not send them."

Servants are included in the commandment. Now this will include household servants as mentioned, but it also includes all other employees as well. We are responsible to see that they also have the opportunity to worship, and are encouraged to do so. They need a day of rest and worship as much as their employer.

God adds one that may seem strange in our day and time, work animals. We do not plow the mule or oxen or horse anymore, or at least seldom. So rare is the use of animals as labor for farming the land today that most of us would give little thought to the need of an animal to rest. Yet, God is concerned for all His creatures, and so should we be. However, if we own pets they may not need a day of rest, for they do not labor, but they do need proper care. Such proper care is surely the present-day thrust of their relation to this command. Cattle, likewise, need to be fed and watered, even on the Lord's Day.

The last one on the list, the "stranger who is within your gate," is one that almost little thought is given to by the present-day Christian. About the only thought would be that this seems to restrict a visitor's freedom. Many would say, "We can't require visitors to conform to our religious habits. In fact, if we are to be proper hosts and hostesses, we must stay home with them and entertain them." God is saying just the opposite. Visitors, in your home on the Lord's Day, must by all means be encouraged to attend the worship of the Lord. By no means should they be allowed to prevent you from worshipping the Lord God. If his being asked to participate in worship restricts the stranger's freedom, it must be remembered that he is also thereby included in the possibility of hope in Christ Jesus. In fact, the only means to win some may well be to insist on their attending worship when they visit your home. If they refuse, then tell them to make themselves comfortable, that you will return when the worship service is concluded. The forgoing was exactly what my mother-in-law would do when visitors came to her home: she always invited them to go with the family to church, but if they would not she simply said, "Well, make yourself at home. We will see you when we return from worship."

"Remember the Sabbath day, to keep it holy." This is the responsibility of the Christian, and it is also the responsibility of the lost. None of God's creation is exempt. But for the keeping of the Sabbath to be meaningful, it must be through faith in the Lord Jesus Christ. It must be kept in love, not out of fear.

# Chapter 6

## Family Obligations

(Exodus 20:12)
"Honor your father and your mother: that your days may be long on the land which the Lord your God gives to you."

### - Introduction -

Now we come to what is called the Transitional Commandment. As you will remember the first four commandments are God-ward in direction. That is, they deal with man's relationship to God. The last five commandments are man-ward in direction. That is, they deal with man's relationship to man. Therefore the Fifth Commandment is the bridge between the two halves; or, as we stated, it is the Transitional Commandment. It is transitional in that it exemplifies both relationships: man to God and man to man.

God's Fatherhood is the archetype of all fatherhood. Paul expressed it this way: "For this cause I bow my knees to the Father of our Lord Jesus Christ, of whom the whole family in heaven and earth is named" (Ephesians 3:14-15). Here is our example of the proper parent-child relationship. In a sense the parent is in the place of God to the child.

The parent is responsible for the life of the child. The parent is responsible for the behavior of the child. In like manner, the child is responsible or answerable to the parent. In that sense the parent-child relationship typifies both halves of the Commandments. Therefore, following this line of thought, we find two things in this Commandment:

### - The Obligation Of The Child To The Parent -

The Commandment says to the child, "Honor your father and your mother." Children are to reverence their parents. Or perhaps a better way to say it would be, "Children show proper respect for your parents." In the reality of the physical sphere of the human body, they created you. They gave of themselves, of their love, that you might live in this world.

What a marvelous opportunity is yours because your parents gave you life and breath. Oh, I have heard all the tales of woe from children who think they have been abused: "I didn't ask to be brought into this world." That may be true, but it is a sad statement to make. Even with all the sin that is in the world, it is still a beautiful world. In spite of all the bad things that happen every day, it is still a privilege to live on this old planet called the Earth that God has given to us. Also, life in this world gives one the opportunity to know God and to become a child of God through faith in Jesus Christ. There is no greater privilege than that of knowing Jesus Christ as Lord and Savior. A child owes his parents for these privileges that come with life.

It is typical of youth to feel restricted by their parents, and to want their freedom. That is exactly what troubled the Prodigal Son in our Lord's parable in Luke 15:11-32. He was tired of all the "do's" and "don'ts" that he lived under in his father's house. He wanted to be free to do his own thing, without someone constantly telling him what to do. It was bad enough for his father to be in charge of his life, but for his older brother to constantly be telling him what to do was simply too much. With the attitude problem exhibited by the older brother (see Luke 15:25-32), it is certainly not taking too much liberty to believe that he would not hesitate to use his position as the elder son and lord it over his younger brother.

The Prodigal wanted his freedom, and he got it. But, oh, he got so much more than he had bargained for! He had not really been ready for the responsibilities that were suddenly thrust on him by his newfound freedom. Before long his money was gone. Then the friends that he had acquired in the far country deserted him, and he was left alone to feed swine for a pagan master. Now his clothes were in rags. Now he was filthy from tending to the hogs. Now there was never enough to eat. Now, when night came, he was so tired that all he could do was fall asleep wherever he could find a place to lay his head. When he awoke in the morning, it was to aching joints and muscles from sleeping on the ground or the floor.

Suddenly he realized that his father's house and control were not such bad things after all. In his father's house even the servants were fed well; they never went hungry. The people he was working for were about to starve him to death. Now he could see how well off he had been in his father's house. Even if he had to go back as a servant in his father's house, it would be far better than where he was. It is a shame to have to discover in this way what a privilege it is to have the life that is given to us by our parents. How much better it is to discover this fact while we still have our parents and our home than to wait until they are gone.

Children are commanded to respect their parents. This includes showing parents proper consideration. God is saying that children should consider their parent's feelings first. Jesus so interpreted this Commandment to the scribes and Pharisees of Jerusalem:

> For God commanded, saying, "Honor your father and mother: and, He who curses father or mother, let him be put to death." But you say, "Whoever shall *say* to his father or his mother, '*It is* a gift, by whatever you may be profited by me;' and does not honor his father or his mother, he shall be free." This way you have made the commandment of God void by your tradition. You hypocrites, well did Isaiah prophesy of you, saying, 'This people draws near to me with their mouth, and honor me with *their* lips; but their heart is far from me. But in vain they are worshipping me, teaching *for* doctrines the commandments of men' (Matthew 15:4-9)

By their tradition they thought they had found a loophole in God's Law. What they were doing was saying, "Everything I own is dedicated to God. Therefore I cannot take care of my aging parents; because my money is no longer mine, it is God's. I can use it for my own needs, but not for anyone else." By their tradition they could ignore the feelings, needs, and wishes of their parents. By their tradition they were trying to nullify the Law of God. By their tradition they were dishonoring their parents and God.

They were also breaking themselves on God's Law. This is what man really does when he is disobedient to God's Law. You see God's Law cannot be broken, only disobeyed. But we can surely break ourselves by our disobedience of it. Here again we see this illustrated in the Prodigal Son. No ship could be more broken, on an ocean reef, than the Prodigal was broken on the reef of sin against God and against his father.

Here children are commanded to hold their parents in high esteem. This simply means to realize their value. Surely their more extended years of experience should warrant the esteem of their children. They have been through the good and the bad times, and know the best choices and directions. Parents are due this esteem not only because of their wisdom, gained through experience, but also because of their love and care for their children. They have fed and fondled, clothed and cradled, romped and rocked, diapered and dandled on the knee, pampered and petted, medicated and bandaged, and whatever else that was needed. Surely such care and love by the parents has earned for them the right to their children's esteem.

Children are to respect their parents because they are their law of life. As your creator, your parents have the right of being your lawgiver, at least until you have reached adulthood. Then, after you have reached your majority, you still owe them honor and respect. This right of the parents to legislate for their children is God-given. We find this truth in God's interpretation of this Fifth Commandment: Deuteronomy 21:18-21:

> If a man has a stubborn and rebellious son, who will not obey the voice of his father, or the voice of his mother, and when they have chastised him, he will still not listen to them: Then his father and his mother shall lay hold on him, and bring him out to the elders of his city, and to the gate of his city; And they shall say to the elders of his city, 'Our son *is* stubborn and rebellious, he will not obey our voice; he *is* a glutton, and a drunkard.' And all the men of his city shall stone him with stones, until he is dead: In this way you will put evil away from among you; and all Israel shall hear, and fear.

This may seem a little stringent; but it is God's choice for a rightly regulated society; it is God's choice for a rightly regulated home; it is God's choice for rightly regulated children. Now it is true that this was for Israel under the Law. It is also true that we now no longer live under the Law, but under grace. Nevertheless, living under grace does not change the basis for God's Law; children are still required to honor their parents, and that includes obedience.

The Apostle Paul gives the proper application of the foregoing phase of this Commandment: "Children, obey your parents in all things: for this is well pleasing to the Lord" (Colossians 3:20). He is saying that "honor" covers more than reverence, respect, and esteem; it is a demand for obedience from the child.

According to Paul, God is saying that when the parents say, "Come," the child is to come, and when the parents say, "Go," the child is to go, and when the parents say "Do," the child is to do, and when they say, "No", the child is to refrain from doing.

Actually this should also include swift, or immediate obedience. In other words, it is not for the child to dawdle or say, "In a minute." The beauty of obedience is in the promptness in which it is done.

But it must be remembered that Paul also added a phrase to this teaching when he wrote to the church at Ephesus: "Children, obey your parents in the Lord: for this is right" (Ephesians 6:1). This adds considerably to the meaning of this Commandment. For now it is seen that obedience is to be done not only in accordance to the will of God, but in the power and strength of God. God can, and will, give all that is needed by the child to be obedient. If this truth could be learned in childhood, how much more blessed would be our adulthood. We need to look to God for strength to do all things, large or small, great or trifling, difficult or simple. We also need to look to God for strength in all situations: in joy or sadness, strength or weakness, health or sickness, success or failure, and any other situation life may lay at our doorstep. Paul really had the answer when he said, "I can do all things through Christ who strengthens me" (Philippians 4:13).

God will also give the child wisdom to know when not to obey their parents, should such a situation arise. If they were to tell the child to lie, steal, murder, or disobey God; then the child is not required to obey. Giving first obedience to God is the higher law.

The Apostle Paul is also the one who tells us that this is "the first commandment with promise" (Ephesians 6:2). Here he is referring to the reading found in Deuteronomy 5:16:

> Honor your father and your mother, as the Lord your God has commanded you; that your days may be prolonged, and that it may go well with you, in the land which the Lord your God gives to you.

The promises, according to Paul, are as follows:

1) "That it may be well with you..."

The idea here is two fold. The first thought is that you will profit from honoring your parent's wisdom. This truth ought to be self-evident, but I think we will do well to make a comment or two concerning it. Loving parents will not deliberately lead you in the wrong way. Experienced parents have passed through the situations that cause the traumas and pains of life. They can therefore aid their children in recognizing the pitfalls of life that their children may miss those bumps and bruises. The second thought is that if children obey the Lord in honoring their parents, then God will bless them for their obedience. If you have the blessings of God, how can you do less than prosper?

2) "...and you may live long on the earth."

The promise is clear: God will bless your obedience by extending your days on earth. There is an illustration of this truth in Jeremiah 35. God there puts the Rechabites to a test. God said to Jeremiah:

> Go to the house of the Rechabites, and speak to them, and bring them to the house of the Lord, to one of the chambers, and give them wine to drink (Jeremiah 35:2).

Jeremiah did as God commanded him:

> And I set before the sons of the house of the Rechabites bowls full of wine, and cups, and I said to them, 'Drink this wine' (Jeremiah 35:5).

To which the Rechabites refused. They had been commanded by their father Jonadab not to drink wine throughout their generations. Also, they were not to build for themselves houses, or plant gardens or vineyards. They were to live in tents and be nomads all their days.

Then Jeremiah said to the Rechabites:

> This is what the Lord of hosts, the God of Israel says to you; 'Because you have obeyed the commandment of Jonadab your father, and kept all his precepts, and done according to all that he has commanded you: Therefore thus says the Lord of hosts, the God of Israel; 'Jonadab the son of Rechab will always have a descendant to serve me forever (Jeremiah 35:18-19).

This is simply God's promise of a long life to the obedient child. Without a question, it pays for children to be obedient to their parents. We are told that it is the beginning of wisdom to heed the commandments of God, and I believe that the following Scriptures have this Fifth Commandment in mind:

> My son do not forget my law; but let your heart keep my commandments: For these shall add length of days, long life, and peace to you (Proverbs 3:1-2).

> To have reverence for the LORD *is* the basis of true wisdom: those who obey His commandments exhibit much wisdom: His praise endures forever (Psalm 111:10)

> Reverence for the LORD is the beginning of knowledge: *but* fools despise wisdom and instruction. My son, hear the instruction of your father, and do not forsake the law of your mother: For they will be an ornament of grace to your head, and chains about your neck (Proverbs 1:7-9).

> Reverence for the LORD *is* the beginning of wisdom: and the knowledge of the Holy One *shows* understanding. For I shall multiply your days, and the years of your life shall be increased (Proverbs 9:10-11).

## - The Obligation Of The Parent To The Child -

We have been discussing reverence, respect, esteem, love, and honor as being due the parent from the child. These things, however, do not come without reason. Such veneration must be earned. The mere fact that you are a biological parent does not in and of itself make you deserve to be so esteemed by your children.

Parents, you must earn honor by living honorably before your children. Now, there is much wrapped up in the term "honorable living." It must include being honest, truthful, and godly in life. If your children hear you tell an untruth of any kind, they will not respect you. If you cheat or steal, they will know that you are not honest. If you do not honor God in your life, then they will learn that you are not a godly person. And when they learn such things from their parents, there is little chance that they will be respectful of their parents or God. One only has to read of the Moabites and Ammonites (the descendants of Lot by his incestuous relationship with his two daughters, Genesis 19:30-38) to see what becomes of children who lose proper veneration of their parents due to the parent's failure to be the right kind of parent.

Several years ago we were forever hearing about a "generation gap." In simple terms, there was a "gap" or separation existing between parents and children. Supposedly this "generation gap" was a barrier to communication between parents and children. It was said that children and parents simply could not speak the same language.

I believe that if there is such a "generation gap" it exists because this Commandment has not been taught. It needs to be taught in Sunday School and preached from the pulpit. It is the obligation of the Lord's churches to teach all His Word. The churches must not fail to teach this truth if it is to be learned by our children. But I believe that the first place for this commandment to be taught is in the homes by parents. God expects this and He commanded it to be done:

> And Moses wrote down this law, and delivered it to the priests, the sons of Levi, who bore the ark of the covenant of the LORD, and to all the elders of Israel. And Moses commanded them, saying, At the end of *every* seven years, in the solemnity of the year of release, during the feast of tabernacles, When all Israel is to come and appear before the LORD your God in the place which He shall choose, you shall read this law before all Israel in their hearing. Gather the people together, men, and women, and children, and the stranger that *is* within your gates, that they may hear, and that they may learn, and reverence the LORD your God, and observe to obey all the words of this law: Do this so that your children, who have not known this law before, may hear, and learn to reverence the LORD your God. Do this as long as you live in the land when you go over Jordan to take possession of it (Deuteronomy 31:9-13).

Concerning this idea, God said of Abraham:

> For I know him, that he will command his children and his household after him, and they shall keep the way of the Lord, to do justice and judgment; that the Lord may bring to pass on Abraham that which He has spoken of him (Genesis 18:19).

You see this was not given as a commandment to Abraham, because God knew that he needed no commandment. Abraham would do this because he loved God.

The Psalmist exemplified this truth, when he said, "Come, you children, listen to me: I will teach you reverence of the Lord" (Psalm 34:11).

The Wise Man expressed this truth when he said, "The just man walks in his integrity: his children are blessed by follow his example" (Proverbs 20:7).

Paul understood this truth because he had learned it by example:

> I am indeed a man who is a Jew, born in Tarsus, a city in Cilicia, yet brought up in this city at the feet of Gamaliel, and taught according to the perfect manner of the law of the fathers, and was zealous toward God, as you all are this day (Acts 22:3).

Paul also reminded Timothy that this was proper:

> And that from a child you have known the holy scriptures, which are able to make you wise unto salvation through faith which is in Christ Jesus (II Timothy 3:15).

On the other hand there is another sense in which this Commandment demands a "Generation Gap." In the eyes of God, parents and children should and do stand on different ground.

God is saying to parents, "Be fathers and mothers to your children." In other words, children do not need buddies and pals to play with. They have plenty of such in their brothers and sisters or friends and classmates. A parent should fill his proper role by maintaining the proper parent-child relationship. Now this is not to say that parents cannot play with their children. Whenever possible parents should play with their children, but such play must be kept within that proper parent-child relationship. There must never be a break down in authority, discipline, and responsibility of the parent in the eyes of the child. Such a break down sets its own warning signs: when the child becomes flippant and sassy or takes too many liberties, beware, because that sacred relationship is being skated on ice that is to thin, and is likely to incur serious complications.

God is also saying to parents, "Let your children be children." A baby is not a teenager, nor is a teenager an adult. There is a solid, responsible reason for each stage in the growth of a child. Parents don't try to thwart the proper stages of development of your child. Don't try to make them old before their time.

Much of the mind-sickness in the world today, without a doubt, can be traced to children being deprived of going through the proper stages of development by over-anxious parents.

Fathers can be guilty of this in the name of wanting their sons to be "real men." They will not show their sons any love or affection from fear that it could make them less of a man. Fathers, if it is all right to hug and kiss your little daughters, then it is all right to hug and kiss your little sons.

Mothers can make as grievous a mistake by wanting their daughters to be popular with the boys. This can be seen when mothers dress their daughters in clothing that is designed for an adult, and allow the use of makeup that is not intended for a child. Too early dating and too much freedom for an immature child can result in tragedy. So, don't try to make your children old before their time. In fact, don't allow them to get old before their time. Let the maturation process that God has built into the system do its own work, in its own time.

God gives us a plain word at this point: "And, you fathers, do not provoke your children to anger" (Ephesians 6:4a). Parents don't give your children reason to rebel against your authority. Be sure that you use the wisdom that age and experience has given you.

Probably the first thing that parents need to remember in this area is that they must be fair with their children. This certainly does not mean that they should give them everything they want. In the first place, in their immaturity they would want things that would be harmful.

A few years back I was passing a pet shop in one of our larger area shopping malls. In the window of that pet shop was a live boa constrictor some six or eight feet long. A child of two or three years of age was at that window. That child was trying his best to get to that snake. When he realized that the snake was on the other side of a glass window he patted on the glass and tried to talk to the snake. There is no question if that child could have gotten his hands on that snake, he would have. There was no fear of that deadly reptile whatsoever. There is also no question that had the child been able to have reached the snake that it would have wrapped itself around the child and crushed the life out of him. It is the nature of boa constrictors to crush living animals into as small and pliable a form as possible and then swallow the animal whole. The child did not know this about the boa constrictor; all he saw was a pretty colored thing crawling around in a glass cage, and he wanted it.

There are many things that children may want that would be just as deadly for them to handle as that boa constrictor would have been for the little child at the pet shop window. Parents must make wise decisions for the children that God has placed in their care. We certainly must not give them everything they want.

Being fair to your children also does not mean letting them do everything they want to do. There are so many things offered to young people today that are simply destructive.

Several years ago, in an area in which I pastored, a man gave his son a brand new Corvette automobile on his birthday. It was something that sixteen-year-old had been telling his father he needed. All the other fellows in his crowd had high-powered cars. Racing those cars was also the "in thing" to do. The father knew this and was so pleased that his son was interested in such things. That same day the teenager took his new car out for a test drive. In less than an hour the highway patrol called the father to tell him that the boy was dead. He had taken the car out on a state highway and opened it up to see how fast it would go. From the report it appears that the car was doing more than 140 miles per hour when one of the front tires hit a rough spot of pavement and the car went airborne for some one hundred feet or more before coming back to the ground. On impact, the car did several rolls before coming to rest on its top. That father gave his son what he wanted, and let him do what he wanted to do. I doubt, however, if that father ever drew another peaceful breath. Parents must be wise in what they allow their children to be involved in.

Well then, if "not provoking your children to wrath," does not mean giving children everything they want, and it does not mean letting them do whatever they want to do, then what does it mean?

First, it means to take time for your children. Take time to listen to them. They need to be heard. If their ideas are good then implement those ideas and express your pleasure at the child for his ingenuity and intelligence. There are many good things we can learn from our children if we will only listen to them.

By the other side of the same token, if your child suggests an idea that is not practical, then tell him and show him why the idea is not a good idea. Under no circumstances should they be put down for their ideas. To do so would be to provoke their wrath.

Under all circumstances explain your judgments to your children. They really do need to know the reasons for your decisions. I for one like to know the why's and why not's of a decision, especially when I am involved in the outcome of that decision. I expect that most people, including children, feel the same way. So when your children ask you "why," tell them. If you cannot explain to them the rationale behind your decisions, you had best reconsider those decisions. It is certain they were not thought out as carefully as they should have been. Parents will also do well to remember that the old answer "Because I said so," is not a sufficient response. The only reply one can expect from that poor excuse for an answer is "wrath," and it will be wrath that was "provoked."

Next, Paul gives some positive and practical advice to parents: "Bring them up in the nurture and admonition of the Lord" (Ephesians 6:4b). No sounder advice has ever been given to parents than this expression of Paul's concerning proper parenting. In the simplest of terms Paul is saying, "Feed your children on the living Word of God." Parents must teach the Word at home. Children cannot be taught the Word in public schools. The church has them such a short time out of each week that it is not possible for them to learn it sufficiently in Sunday School or Worship Services or other organizations of the church. The home is the best place to teach them the Word as we have covered earlier in the chapter.

Paul's last advice also means that parents should correct their children with the Word of God. Be careful here! This does not mean to use the Word like a whip. A woman I once knew made her children read long passages of Scripture as punishment. That only accomplished making the Word hateful to the children. It certainly did not make the children better. But if the Word can be applied to the situation, and it always applies, then it can be most effective in proper correction of the child's ways. The Psalmist said, "Your word is a lamp to my feet, and a light to my path" (Psalm 119:105). This also means to take God's example in proper parenting, for He is the Supreme example of a parent. He is always correct in His dealings with His children.

The keeping of this Commandment is not easy for children or parents, but with God's help it can be accomplished. Therefore let us dedicate ourselves to being obedient to the will of God in this matter.

# Chapter 7

## The Sacredness Of Man's Life

(Exodus 20:13)
"You shall not murder."

### - Introduction -

That there be no misunderstanding as to the subject at hand: "kill" in the Hebrew is the word "ratsach" which is translated "to kill, (a human being) especially to murder." Murder is that deliberate act of depriving another human being of their life. In order to reach a complete understanding of "You shall not murder" we need to narrow down the subject by definition:

### - Murder Defined -

Webster's New Twentieth Century Dictionary says murder is "The unlawful and premeditated killing of one human being by another; also, any killing done while committing some other felony, as rape or robbery."

I understand the full intent of this definition because my father-in-law was murdered. One cold February day, more than twenty-two years ago, my father-in-law was working in a gas station in a small South Georgia town along Interstate 75. At about 11 a.m. someone drove in to get gas. My father-in-law had evidently been filling the tanks of several semi trucks at the diesel pumps, some fifty yards or so from the gasoline pumps. It seems evident that someone drove up to the gas pumps in an automobile so he did not take time to put the money from the diesel sales in the cash register. He filled the automobile tank and made change for the person with money he had received from the truck drivers. The driver of the car saw what appeared to be a rather large wad of money and shot and killed and robbed my father-in-law. Whoever the person or persons was, for they were never caught, wanted the money and did not mind killing to get it. They shot and killed my father-in-law for what was later determined to be less than five hundred dollars. This fits the dictionary definition: there was the intent to commit a crime. There was the use of a deadly weapon with destructive force. A life was destroyed unlawfully. It was cold blooded, murder for profit.

The foregoing is just one of several types of murder that must be considered in order to understand this Sixth Commandment. God's Word deals with all types of murder. God is also explicit concerning what murder is, and how it should be dealt with. We will begin with murder by malice.

## (Murder By Malice)

Murder by malice is the type of killing most commonly associated with murder. Concerning this type of murder, the Bible says:
> If a man deliberately pushes another man out of hatred, or in hatred deliberately throws an object at him, or in hatred deliberately strikes him with his fist, and that man dies: he that struck him shall surely be put to death; for he *is* a murderer: the murdered person's nearest relative shall execute the murderer, when he finds him (Numbers 35:20-21).

Murder by malice fits the classic dictionary definition of murder. There is the use of a deadly weapon (instrument of iron, stone, a wooden club, or a fist) with destructive force. In every situation malice motivates the act ("out of hatred" or "in hatred strikes"). It is obvious that each situation is planned ("deliberately").

## (Murder By Criminal Neglect)

Mostly we do not think of it as possible for negligence to carry with it the charge of murder. However we have a responsibility to our fellowman for his safety. We really are our brother's keepers. God's Word makes this responsibility clear:
> When you build a new house, then you shall make a wall of protection around the roof, that you do not bring blood on your house should any man fall from there (Deuteronomy 22:8).

If we fail to take proper care in building our house and that negligence results in the injury or death of an individual, we are responsible. Suppose that you use a gas space heater in your home and do not properly vent it, and members of your family are overcome by the fumes; you bear the responsibility. If they die, you are guilty of manslaughter. That is one type of criminal neglect. God's Word bears this out:
> If men physically fight with each other, and a pregnant woman is hurt, and the child is born prema-

turely, and yet no harm follows: Then the one who is responsible for the harm shall be surely pay for the harm done, according to what the woman's husband and the judges shall *determine*. And if the harm done results in death, then the responsible party shall be executed (Exodus 21:22-23).

The above reference is somewhat different than the one preceding it. This is a case of the innocent bystander being killed. For instance, if you get in your automobile and start down the highway and go to sleep at the wheel and run over someone and kill them, that is manslaughter. There was no intent to kill; there was no malice, there is only criminal neglect.

Let's look at a similar case but with a different twist. If you drink alcohol and get behind the wheel of an automobile and run over someone and kill him or her, it is murder. You say, "That does not fit the criteria for murder, there is no malice." Oh, but it does. Perhaps there is no hate, but there is intent. To drive under the influence of alcohol shows the intent. It is a deliberate breaking of the law to drive under the influence of alcohol. To do so violates the right of pedestrians to walk in safety on our streets. It is not only criminal neglect it is also murder.

The foregoing Scripture reference also refers to feticide by criminal neglect. If a woman is deliberately caused to abort her unborn child and the child dies, it is considered by God's Word to be murder, requiring that "the responsible party shall be executed."

If taking the life of an unborn child is feticide, then abortion will necessarily fall into the same category since it is the willful and deliberate taking of the life of an unborn child.

Let us suppose that a woman is pregnant and does not want the child. If she then deliberately does something to cause the baby to be aborted then it is murder. The only difference in this case is it is not murder by criminal neglect; it is murder by deliberate choice.

Now, let us suppose another scenario. A woman is pregnant and does not want the child, so she goes to an abortionist and has the child aborted it is murder by choice and it is murder for hire. All the elements of murder for hire are present.

If an ox gores a man or a woman, and they die: then the ox shall surely be destroyed, and his flesh shall not be eaten; but the owner of the ox shall be free of any guilt of its actions. But if the ox tended to thrust with his horn in times past, and its owner has been informed of such tendencies, and he has not kept him shut up, and a man or a woman is killed; the ox shall be destroyed, and its owner shall also be put to death (Exodus 21:28-29).

The above is a third type of criminal neglect. Let us suppose, for the sake of illustration, that you own a Pit Bulldog that is known to be dangerous, but you allow it to run loose anyway. If that dog attacks a person and kills them you are guilty of murder by criminal neglect.

### (Murder For Hire)

Now we come to a completely different type of murder. Murder for hire is the case of a person wanting someone killed and hiring a third person to do the murder. The Bible says the following about this type of murderer: "Cursed is the man who hires himself out to murder an innocent person. And all the people shall say, Amen" (Deuteronomy 27: 25).

In this type of murder both parties are guilty of murder, the one who hires the murderer and the one who actually does the killing. Look at the one who hires the murder done: He is guilty by reason of his malice and/or planning and use of a dangerous weapon (the one hired). All the elements that make up murder are present. Now, the one hired is just as guilty of murder: His malice is replace by greed, which acts out the same result. He makes his preparations and carries them out. Again all the elements of murder are present.

### (Murder By Perjury)

Murder by perjury is a dreadful type of murder. It takes its form from the father of murder: Satan, himself. That form is in a lie.

> If a false witness comes forward to testify against any man of committing a wrong doing; Then both the men, between whom the controversy has arisen shall stand before the LORD, before the priests, and the judges, who serve the Lord in those days. Then the judges shall make diligent investigation into the matter: and if the witness is found to be a false witness, and has testified falsely against his brother; Then you shall do to him, as he had planned to have done to his brother: in this way you shall put away such evil from among you (Deuteronomy 19:16, 18-19).

A person is accused of a crime punishable by death. Now it happens that the person is innocent. However, a witness comes forward and testifies falsely that the accused is guilty. If the accused is convicted and executed for the crime, then the witness who perjured himself is guilty of murder.

The murder of Naboth the Jezreelite, recorded in I Kings 21:4-18 is one of the clearest cases of murder by perjury that I know of:

One day Ahab, the king of Israel, came home in a terrible rage. He wanted a plot of land owned by a man from Jezreel, named Naboth, and the man would not sell his land. Ahab, like a little child, went to bed and would not eat he was on such a pout. When Queen Jezebel heard that Ahab was in his room pouting, she wanted to know why he was so upset. Ahab told her about trying to buy Naboth's vineyard and Naboth's refusal to sell. In my mind I can hear the diabolical laughter of queen Jezebel when she heard Ahab's problem. Then she said, "Well, what is your problem? You are the king of Israel, are you not? Get up and eat and be happy. I will get the vineyard for you." So she wrote letters in Ahab's name and sealed them with the royal seal, and sent them to the elders and nobles at Jezreel. In the letters she instructed them to call the people together for a time of prayer and fasting, and set Naboth in a place of honor among the people. They were to hire two worthless men and seat them across from Naboth and have them witness against him, saying that he had blasphemed God and the king. Then they were to take Naboth out and stone him to death. The leaders at Jezreel did as the queen commanded, and then they sent word, to her, that Naboth was dead. Jezebel then told Ahab to get up and go take possession of Naboth's vineyard. Here we have an open and shut case of murder by perjury, but it is also clear-cut case of murder for hire, and murder for profit.

## (Murder By City/State Responsibility)

I have never heard of a case of murder by city or state responsibility being prosecuted. It involves the charge of murder being brought against a city, county, state, or national government. The Word of God states the situation as follows:

> If someone is found murdered lying in a field in the land which the LORD your God is giving you as a possession, *and* it is not known who has murdered him: then your leaders and your judges shall come and measure from the body to the cities which *are* around the murdered man. And it shall be, that the leaders of the city, which is nearest the murdered man shall take a young cow, which has not been trained to pull a plow; and they shall bring the young cow to a valley, which has not been plowed or planted, and they shall behead the heifer there in the valley. Then the priests the sons of Levi shall come near; for they are the ones whom the

LORD your God has chosen to minister to him, to pronounce blessings in His name, and to settle every disagreement and to determine every punishment that shall be carried out. And all the leaders of the city, that are nearest to the murdered man, shall present themselves to the priests, and they shall wash their hands over the heifer that has been beheaded in the valley. And they shall swear by these words, 'We have not committed this murder, neither have we seen the one who did commit this murder. Be merciful, O LORD, to your people Israel, whom You have redeemed, and do not charge Your people with the guilt of murdering this innocent person.' And they shall not be charged with the murder. When you follow these instructions, doing what is right in the Lord's eyes, you shall be cleansed of the guilt of murder in your city (Deuteronomy 21:1-9).

To illustrate this type of murder we will have to create a situation. Suppose that a certain city government has knowledge of criminal activities within its city limits. The city government is responsible to dispose of such an element. However if the city officials ignore this menace to society, and a citizen loses his life because of those criminal activities then that city is responsible for that loss of life. The charge would be murder due to criminal neglect of responsibility by the city government.

## - God Considers Man's Life Is Sacred -

If anything is certain, it is that God considers man's life sacred. From the beginning to the end of His Word we are taught this truth. The following passages illustrate clearly how highly God values the life of man:

And the LORD said to Cain, Where *is* your brother Abel? And Cain said, 'How should I know: *Am* I responsible for my brother's welfare?' And He said, 'What have you done? The voice of your brother's blood cries out to Me from the ground! And now the earth, which has opened its mouth to receive your brother's blood from your hand, curses you; when you plow the ground, it will no longer yield to you its abundance; and you shall wanderer the earth, as a fugitive all the days of your life (Genesis 4:9-12).

You shall not eat the flesh if any animal with its

life, which is the blood, still in it. And you can be sure that I will require the blood of your lives at the hand of every beast, and at the hand of man; at the hand of every man's brother will I require the life of man. Whoever sheds man's blood, by man shall his blood be shed: for God created man in His Own image." (Genesis 9:4-6)

You shall not commit murder (Exodus 20:13, Deuteronomy 5:17).

You shall not commit murder (Romans 13:9)

And if a man strikes another man with an instrument of iron, and he dies, that man *is* a murderer: the murderer shall surely be put to death. And if a man picks up a stone and strikes another man, and that man dies, he *is* a murderer: the murderer shall surely be put to death. Or *if* a man strikes another man with a wooden club, and he dies, that man *is* a murderer: the murderer shall surely be put to death. The murdered person's nearest relative shall execute the murderer: when he finds him, he shall execute him. If a man deliberately pushes another man out of hatred, or in hatred deliberately throws an object at him, or in hatred deliberately strikes him with his fist, and that man dies: he that struck him shall surely be put to death; for he is a murderer: the murdered person's nearest relative shall execute the murderer, when he finds him (Numbers 35:16-21).

Anyone who murders another person shall be put to death. They shall only be sentenced to death by the testimony of witnesses: but the testimony of one witness shall not be sufficient to result in the death penalty (Numbers 35:30).

Cursed is the one who murders his neighbor secretly. And all the people shall say, 'Amen.' Cursed is the one who murders an innocent person for money. And all the people shall say, 'Amen' (Deuteronomy 27:24-25).

Whoever hates his brother is a murderer, and you know that no murderer has eternal life abiding in him (I John 3:15).

But the fearful, and unbelieving, and the abominable, and murderers, and whoremongers, and sorcerers, and idolaters, and all liars, shall have their part in the lake of fire and brimstone: which is the second death (Revelation 21:8).

Blessed *are* those who keep His commandments that they may have the right to the tree of life, and that they may enter through the gates into the city. But all evil persons: sorcerers, the sexually immoral, murderers, idolaters, and whoever loves and practices telling lies are not allowed in God's holy city (Revelation 22:15).

So, from Genesis to Revelation, God speaks to us concerning how He views murder and the murderer. With this in mind let us take a serious look at the faces of murder and the truth of the terrible penalty God says the murderer must pay.

## - The Definition Applied To Some Specific Cases -

The elder of the first pair of brothers (Cain) learned to his sorrow the penalty God says a murderer must pay. The story of Cain and Abel is recorded in Genesis 4:3-16. According to that history, Cain and Abel both offered a sacrifice to God. Cain's offering was of the fruit of the ground; he was a farmer. Abel's offering was of the firstlings of the flock: a lamb. He was a shepherd. Abel's offering was acceptable to God and Cain's was not.

The evidence is that these men knew the Law of Atonement for sin. God had established that Law when their parents sinned, in the Garden of Eden, and God covered their nakedness with the coats made from the skins of animals (Genesis 3:21). Throughout the Bible it is taught that by the shedding of blood, atonement is made for sin. God slew the animals, shedding their blood, to cover the sin of Adam and Eve. Cain knew this but did not practice it. He did not see that he needed to offer a sacrifice for sin. He evidently thought that he had no sin and that he needed no atonement. He offered only a tenants offering to God. He recognized that he owed God for what he had produced on the land, but did not see his need to make a sin offering. Therefore his offering to God was unacceptable. Abel knew the Law, and saw himself as a sinner in need of atonement, so he offered a blood sacrifice to God for his sin; therefore, God received his sacrifice as worthy.

When we pick up the story, we find Cain is terribly angry with God because his sacrifice was not accepted (Genesis 4:5). As God always does with man, He tried to reason with Cain (Genesis 4:6-7). Cain listened but he did not hear. What do you do when you are angry with God? You certainly cannot assault God. So, when Cain was alone with Abel, his rage against God manifested itself against his brother. After all, it was his brother that showed him up; he was surely the one who should receive the blast of Cain's anger. Cain killed his brother and then hid his body in a grave (Genesis 4:8, 11).

There we see anger leading to hate which resulted in the planning and intentional killing of Abel. That makes it murder. You may say, "Wait just a minute! Where is the disobedience to the law on Cain's part? Up to this point we read of no law against murder being given." Actually, what we do not find concerning law, at this point, is that no set penalty for murder is given. When we look closely at the story, we see Cain burying Abel. There can be only one purpose in this: to conceal the deed. If the mind must hide the deed, then it is because the mind knows that the deed is wrong. If the mind knows that the deed is wrong, then that knowledge becomes the law concerning the deed. Paul speaks to this type of knowing the law in Romans 2:12-16:

> For all who sin without knowing God's Law will perish, because of their sin, even though they do not have God's Law; just as all who sin knowing the Law will be judged by the Law. For it is not those who hear the Law that *are* justified before God, but those who obey the Law: they are the ones who shall be justified. For when the Gentiles, who do not have the Law, practice by nature the things taught in the Law, though they do not have the Law, are a law to themselves: which is evidence that the Law is written in their hearts. Their own conscience also bears witness that their thoughts either accuse or else excuse the deeds they do. The day is coming when God will judge the secret life of every man by Jesus Christ according to my gospel.

Cain's act against his brother Abel was murder, and it was the first recorded murder.

Jacob also recognized the truth that God will not tolerate the murder of one human by another. He had to deal with a crisis that brought him and his family face to face with a situation in which his sons placed themselves above God and His law.

When we study the story of the killing of Shechem and his fellow townsmen by Simeon and Levi (Genesis 34:11-29), there seems to be a completely different situation in that sad story. It would appear on the surface that this was justifiable homicide. In fact, this is what Simeon and Levi called it (Genesis 34:31). As far as they were concerned, they were simply being good brothers by defending their sister's honor. However, that does not relieve them of the charge of murder. This is clear from what we read in

Deuteronomy 22:28-29:

> If a man takes a young woman who is a virgin, who is not engaged to be married, and rapes her and it is discovered; Then the man that raped her shall give to the young woman's father fifty shekels of silver, and she shall be his wife; because he violated her, he may not divorce her as long as he lives.

This was evidently the custom of the times, which later God incorporated into His law. With all of his heart, Shechem wanted Dinah to be his wife: Genesis 34:3-4 say, "His soul was strongly attracted to Dinah the daughter of Jacob, and he loved the young woman, and spoke kindly to the her. And Shechem spoke to his father Hamor, saying, Get me this girl for me to marry." This is also obvious from his willingness to do whatever her brothers required of him to marry her Genesis 34:11-19:

> And Shechem said to Dinah's father and to her brothers, "Let me find favor in your sight, and whatever you shall ask of me I will give. Ask of me as much dowry and gifts you may desire, and I will give whatever it is that you require of me: but give me the young woman to be my wife." And the sons of Jacob answered Shechem and Hamor his father deceitfully, because he had defiled Dinah their sister: And they said to them, "We cannot do what you ask. For us to give our sister to one that is uncircumcised would bring reproach on us. But we will give our consent for you to marry her, if all of your males will be circumcised as we are. This is the only way we will give our daughters to you to marry. And if you do this we will take your daughters to us in marriage, we will dwell with you, and we will become one people. But if you will not do as we say, and be circumcised; then will we take our daughter, and we will be gone." And their words pleased Hamor, and Shechem Hamor's son. And the young man did not delay to do what they asked him to do, because he found Jacob's daughter delightful, and he *was* more honorable than all of his father family.

From the foregoing passage it is obvious that Shechem tried to fulfill the custom concerning a virgin. He would have married and cared for Dinah as a true and faithful husband, therefore, Simeon and Levi cannot be justified for what they did.

Before his death Jacob settled the guilt of Simeon and Levi, when he

said:
> Simeon and Levi *are* brothers; instruments of cruelty dwell in their hearts. O my soul, do not listen to their advice; do not let my honor be trusted to them. For in anger they murdered a man, and in their willfulness they destroyed a household. Let their anger be cursed, for it was brutal; and their wrath, for it was cruel: I will divide their inheritance in Jacob, and scatter them among the tribes of Israel (Genesis 49:5-7).

What they did was not in defense of Dinah, but to satisfy their own need for vengeance. They hated Shechem for what he had done to their sister. They planned and carried out his execution. They knew what they did was wrong. What they did fits the criteria for murder. Therefore, they were murderers

David, the sweet singer of the Psalms, the warrior King of Israel, looked down from his roof into an adjoining courtyard and saw a young woman bathing. She was the most beautiful woman David had ever seen; at least in his mind this must have been so. Instead of going back into his room and tending to his own business, he made inquiries concerning her. That was his first sin. When he found out that she was a married woman, for she was the wife of Uriah the Hittite, he should have, without question, gone on about his business and left her alone. Instead he sent for her, took her, and committed adultery with her. He was the king. He could do what he wanted. At least this is how he must have justified in his own mind what he did. However, regardless of what he thought, these were his second and third sins.

Sometime passed and David received a message from Bathsheba saying that she was pregnant with his child. Up to this point David probably thought that he could hide his sin. Now the fat was in the fire! Now he knew that hiding his sin would be very difficult if not impossible. He knew the Law was explicit concerning adultery:
> And the man that commits adultery with *another* man's wife – the wife of his neighbor, the adulterer and the adulteress shall surely be put to death (Leviticus 20:10).

What was he to do? He could have sought God's mind in the matter and faced whatever the Lord instructed, even if it meant death. He also could have faced Uriah and taken the consequences. He did neither.

While David was having this adulteress affair with Bathsheba in Jerusalem, Uriah, her husband, was away with the Israeli army defending the kingdom's honor against the Ammonites. David sent word to Joab, the commander of the army to send Uriah to him. David thought that he could have Uriah return to his home and wife while in Jerusalem, and when he found out that Bathsheba was pregnant, he would think it was his child. However, instead of going home to his wife Uriah slept in the servant's quarter at the king's house. David called Uriah in and asked him why he had not gone home to his wife. Uriah answered David saying, "The Ark, and the armies of Israel, and Judah, are living in tents; and my lord Joab, and the servants of my lord, are encamped in the open fields; shall I then go into my house, to eat and to drink, and to lie with my wife? *As* you live, and *as* your soul lives, I will not do this thing" (II Samuel 11:11).

Now what was David to do? You can be sure he did as all sinners do; he continued to try to hide his sin. He invited Uriah to eat and drink with him and he got Uriah drunk thinking that now he would go home to Bathsheba. But again, he did not do that. He slept in the servant's quarters again.

At this point things were getting desperate for David. He had to do something, and he had to do it quickly. So he ordered Uriah back to the battlefield and sent with him a note to Joab, the commander of the army, to have him killed in battle. He instructed Joab to put Uriah in the hottest part of the battle and to then withdraw from him, leaving him alone to die at the hand of the enemy. With this act David added murder to his list of personal sins. This is not my interpretation; this is God's judgment on David:

> Why have you despised the commandment of the Lord, to do evil in His sight? You have killed Uriah the Hittite with the sword, and have taken his wife *to be* your wife, and have slain him with the sword of the children of Ammon (II Samuel 12:9).

David was a murderer, plain and simple. He could make no excuse for his deed. He openly admitted that he was guilty as charged when he said, "I have sinned against the Lord" (II Samuel 12:13). You can read the entire sordid affair in II Samuel chapters 11-12.

With this we come to what the Bible sets out to be done with the murderer.

## - The Penalty For Murder -

Cain had perpetrated a terrible wrong, when he murdered his brother Abel, and he had to realize the seriousness of his crime and that it was evil. God came and faced him with his deed:

> And the Lord said to Cain, "Where *is* your brother Abel?" And he said, "I do not know: *am* I my brother's keeper?" And God said, "What have you done? The

voice of your brother's blood cries out to me from the ground" (Genesis 4:9-10).

To further drive home the enormity of his hateful act, God said to him, "When you plow the ground, it will no longer yield its strength to you" (Genesis 4:11).

Then God laid out the extent of that curse: "From now on you will be a fugitive and a vagabond in the earth" (Genesis 4:12).

At this point I think Cain would have preferred that God had pronounced the death penalty on him. In his anguish Cain cried out, "My punishment is greater than I can bear" (Genesis 4:13).

From this time forward he knew that the hand of all men would be against him. Never again would he know a peaceful day or night. All of his days would be spent in looking over his shoulder in fear, always expecting to be struck down by the "avenger of blood." All of his nights would be filled with dreadful dreams. He would continually relive his terrible deed in those dreams. I am sure that the awful nightmares, created by the murder he had committed, stayed with him all of his nights for all of his many years.

His deed exacted another toll on his life. The one thing he loved most was taken from him. He would never again be able to successfully farm the land. The earth that had swallowed his brother's blood would no longer yield its blessings to him (Genesis 4:12). Besides, as a "fugitive and a vagabond," there would be no way for him to farm the land again; he would never be in one place long enough. He had forfeited all that was worthwhile to him. I suspect that there were many times he wished for death to take him out of his misery. But even death was denied him until he had served his sentence to the full.

## - The Penalty For Murder Changed Under The Law -

After the flood God allowed man to eat meat as well as fruits and vegetables. Up to this time all humans and animals were vegetarians:
> And God said, "Behold, I have given you every plant that produces grain, and the fruit of every tree that has its seed in it shall be food for you. And to every beast of the earth, and to every fowl of the air, and to everything that lives on the earth, in which there is life, to them I have given every green plant for food." So all that He said came to pass" (Genesis 1:29-30).

For the first time there would be carnivorous animals roaming the earth. The shedding of blood became something that was done to maintain life for both man and beast:

> And God blessed Noah and his sons, and said to them, "Be fruitful, and multiply, and repopulate the earth. And you will be feared and cause terror to every beast of the earth, and to every fowl of the air, to all that move on the earth, and to all the fish in the sea; they are delivered into your control. They shall all be food for you now even as I previously gave you green plants for food. But you shall not eat the flesh of any animal or any fowl with its life, which is the blood, still in it" (Genesis 9:1-4).

With the shedding of blood to obtain food came the potential of man shedding the blood of man and animals shedding the blood of men. So other things had to also change. God saw that there had to be something done to protect men from each other, and to exact justice on any man or animal who would kill a man so He changed the penalty for murder:

> And from every beast, from every man, and from every man's brother I will certainly require a price for shedding the lifeblood of man. Whoever sheds man's blood shall have his blood shed by man: for man was created in the image of God (Genesis 9:5-6).

It is not sufficient that one generation or one people know that murder is wrong, and that God will not tolerate the deed. So He passed the law down to the heads of the new race of mankind. This law is not for one family or nation, but for the entire human race.

Here God emphasizes the heinousness of the crime by adding the penalty of "a life for a life." In plain and simple terms, God says that from this point on the murderer will forfeit his life. Therefore, if a man chooses to murder another man, he has chosen to give up his own life. So the murderer becomes judge and jury over his own life. He chooses his own fate. He is responsible for his own death.

Jacob understood the penalty for murder and said to his sons, Simeon and Levi:

> You have caused me much distress, and you have made me disgusting to the Canaanites and the Perizzites who inhabitants the land. And since I am few in number, they will gather themselves together against me, and slay me; and my family and I will be destroyed. (Genesis 34:30).

Just before he died, Jacob called his sons to him and told them what was to be their future. Of Simeon and Levi he said:

> Simeon and Levi *are* brothers; instruments of cru-

> elty dwell in their hearts. O my soul, do not listen to their advice; do not let my honor be trusted to them. For in anger they murdered a man, and in their willfulness they destroyed a household. Let their anger be cursed, for *it was* brutal; and their wrath, for it was cruel: I will divide their inheritance in Jacob, and scatter them among the tribes of Israel (Genesis 49:5-7).

They would not share in the division of the Promised Land. They must be content to live within the territory of their brothers. Simeon had to share in the inheritance of Judah, and Levi was scattered throughout the twelve tribes of Israel.

God spared their lives, but they had to live with the memory of their crime all the days of their lives. Their descendants have also lived with the memory of their ancestors' crime to this day. So it shall ever be.

## - The Law Made Judgment For Murder More Specific -

With the giving of His Law, God becomes exceedingly specific. Over and over again, from Genesis to Revelation He says that murder is to brings death to the murderer: Genesis 9:5; Exodus 21:12; Leviticus 24:17; Numbers 35:16-21; Ezekiel 16:38; Ezekiel 22:4; Habakkuk 2:17; Romans 13:9-10; Revelation 19:2. The foregoing references are but a few of the total number of verses that prohibit murder or state the penalty for murder.

God also makes it plain to understand that we are not to pity the murderer:

> If any man hates his neighbor, and lies in wait for him, and rise up against him, and strikes him mortally and he dies, and then the murderer flees to one of the cities of refuge: The officials of his home town shall have him brought back from there, and they shall deliver him into the hands of those charged with the execution of murderers, that he may be put to death. You shall not feel sorry for him, but you shall purge Israel from the guilt of innocent blood, only then all will go well with you (Deuteronomy 19:11-13).

Here are all the ingredients of the classic murder: Notice there is malice. The account says there is "hate" for the victim. Then we are told that there is intent. This is evident in that the killer lay "in wait." The "lying in wait" establishes the fact that the killing was planned. Next there is the taking of the life. The killer struck his victim and he died. Finally there is the breaking of the Law. This is clear from the statement that he may be taken prisoner and turned over to those charged with the execution of murderers so that he can be put to death. If ever Scripture was clear, it is in the point that the murderer must die.

Because murder is a willful crime, there must be no sympathy, for the killer: "You shall not feel sorry for him." To sympathize with a murderer is to approve of his crime and therefore to makes the one who sympathizes with the murderer an accomplice to the crime.

The word is also explicit in that no ransom may be accepted for the murderer: "Also you shall not accept a ransom for the life of a murderer, who has been sentenced to death: but he shall be certainly put to death" (Number 35:31). No fine may be paid nor can anything substitute for the death penalty: The murderer must die for his crime. This is the judgment of God on the murderer.

## - The Penalty Under The New Testament -

Some may object that these are all Old Testament teachings, saying that Christ taught differently in the New Testament. Did the Lord really teach contrary to Old Testament Law? Let's look at what the Lord said and see if this is true:

> You have heard that it was said to our people by Moses, 'You shall not murder; and whoever commits murder shall be subject to judgment: But I say to you, that whoever is angry with his brother without a cause shall be subject to judgment: and whoever shall say to his brother, 'You are an empty, worthless, good for nothing,' shall be answerable to the Sanhedrin. But whoever shall say to anyone, 'You fool,' shall be in danger of hell fire. (Matthew 5:21-22).

Actually, what the Lord is teaching here is the spirit of the Law. He is going right to the core of the matter and says that hate is at the root of murder. In no way does this deny the penalty for murder. A good exposition of what Jesus is teaching in Matthew 5:21-22 is found in Mark 7, where He says:

> It is the things, which come out of the heart of man that make him unclean. For from within, out of the heart of men, come evil thoughts, adulteries and other sexually immoral practices, murders, stealing, greed, cruelty, deceitfulness, vulgarity, slander, arrogance, and lack of judgment: All these evil things come from within, and make the man unclean (Mark 7:20-23).

He is not denying the Mosaic Law, He is simply stating the reason for the Law being given: Evil desires that originate in the heart are the cause of murder and every other evil deed. In fact He plainly says that to be angry with one's brother will make you answerable to judgment in the same way as murder, because it is that evil thought that leads to murder.

John expresses the same idea in I John 3:15: "Whoever hate his brother is a murderer: and you know that no murderer has eternal life abiding in him." He is saying that the one who holds hate in his heart deserves the same judgment that the murderer does.

## - The Penalty And God's Right To Vengeance -

Those who object to the Old Testament Law of Capital Punishment often raise another question, "Doesn't God's Word teach that man is not to take vengeance, only God has that right?" The answer to that is "yes" and "no." *Yes*, it does say that vengeance is the Lord's business. *No*, it does not say that man is not to carry out the law of capital punishment. The references is as follows:

> Vengeance and recompense are Mine. The sinner's foot will slip in due time: for their day of calamity is near by, and the things that will happen to them will come in a hurry. For the LORD shall judge His people, and He will have pity on His servants, when He sees that their power is gone, and there is none shut up, or left (Deuteronomy 32:35-36).

> You shall not hold hatred for your brother in your heart: you shall rebuke your neighbor when he goes wrong, and not allow sin to remain in him. You shall not avenge, nor bear any grudge against the children of your people, but you shall love your neighbor as yourself: I AM the LORD (Leviticus 19:17-18).

The teaching as expressed in the first verse says clearly that vengeance belongs to God alone. The second verse is teaching the proper conduct of brother-to-brother, friend-to-friend, and neighbor-to-neighbor. It is personal behavior between individuals that is under consideration. Certainly it is teaching that we are not to mistreat one another in any way. Therefore neither of these verses teaches for or against the enforcement of capital punishment by society on it members.

The first verse also speaks of judgment falling from God on His people because of their sin of rebellion against Him. It is not dealing with the sins of man against society. Nor does it speak of the penalty for such crimes.

In the following verses Paul is explaining the proper conduct of Christians in relation to the world around them. He is telling them how they are to live before the lost in witness of what Christianity is all about. We are to let the peoples of this world know that our lives have been changed from darkness to light. Again, as in the verses preceding these verses, he is not dealing with the carrying out of social laws.

> Do not repay any man with evil things when he does evil things to you. Live an honest life before all men. If it is possible, as far as you are responsible, live peacefully with all men. Dearly beloved, do not avenge yourselves, but rather allow God's wrath to have control: for it is written, Vengeance *is* mine; I will repay, says the Lord. Therefore if your enemy is hungry feed him; if he is thirsty, give him something to drink: for when you do this you will pour coals of fire on his head. Do not allow evil to overcome you, but overcome evil with good (Romans 12:17-21).

The writer of the book of Hebrews, in the following verses, is expounding the truth concerning our relationship to God in grace.

> But remember the former days, in which, after you came into the light of Christ, you endured a great test that came to you in the form of afflictions. Sometimes you were publicly humiliated and persecuted; and sometimes you stood shoulder to shoulder those who were treated as you were. For you had compassion on me while I was in prison, and joyfully accepted the confiscation of your property, because you were aware in your heart that you have better and more lasting possessions in heaven (Hebrews 10:32-34).

As he says in Verse 26, "If we deliberately continue to sin after we have heard a full understanding of the truth, (after we have heard and understood the truth about Jesus, if we willfully reject Him as Savior) then there is no sacrifice for sins left for us." Then God will take vengeance on such. So, this passage, like the others is not dealing with social laws or their enforcement. Nowhere in God's Word do we find anything that says we should not enforce the death penalty for murder. It is not found in the teachings of the Old Testament or the New Testament.

## - The Reasons For The Penalty -

## (Man Created In The Image Of God)

God said, "You shall not kill," and "Whoever sheds man's blood, shall have his blood shed by man..." Then He gives us the reason, "...for in the image of God He created man" (Genesis 9:6).

Man is God's crowning creation. He made man higher than the sun, moon, stars and the earth. Nothing in the material creation compares with man. God placed man over all of His creation:

> And God blessed them, and God said unto them, 'Be fruitful, and multiply, and replenish the earth, and subdue it: and have dominion over the fish of the sea, and over the fowl of the air, and over every living thing that moves upon the earth' (Genesis 1:28).

God placed man above the angels. I know that more translations of the Bible, than not, say that God made man "a little lower than the angels" as we find in the following passages:

> What is man, that You are care so much for him? And the son of man, that You have fellowship with him? For You have made him a little lower than the angels, and have crowned him with glory and honor. You gave him dominion over the works of Your hands; You have put all of creation under his control: All sheep and oxen, yes, and the beasts of the field; The birds of the air, and the fish in the sea, and whatever swims in the waters of the oceans (Psalm 8:4-8).

However the word in this passage translated "angel" is the Hebrew word "el-o-heem," which is usually translated "God." There are four translations (The Revised Standard Version, The American Standard Version, The New Living Translation, and The New American Standard Version) that translate it as "God." Let me quote from one of the four:

> What is man that You take thought of him, And the son of man that You care for him? Yet You have made him a little lower than God, And You crown him with glory and majesty! You make him to rule over the works of Your hands; You have put all things under his feet, All sheep and oxen, And also the beasts of the field, The birds of the heavens and the fish of the sea, Whatever passes through the paths of the seas (Psalm 8:4-8, NASB).

Evidently the other translators took up the Jewish tradition of translating this passage to read "a little lower than the angels."

I also recognize that all translators of the New Testament make Hebrews 2:7-8 quote Psalm 8:4-8 as follows:

> You made him a little lower than the angels; You crowned him with glory and honor, and set him over the works of your hands: You have put all of your creation in his absolute control. For when God put all things in his control, He left nothing that is not in his control. But now we do not at this time see all things put in his control.

I believe they are translating Jewish tradition in this instance rather than a literal translation of the Hebrew word "el-o-heem'." For this reason I believe that man was made "a little lower than God," not "a little lower than angels."

If the word should be translated "angel" it should only be done so in a limited sense. The angels were not made in the image of God. The angels cannot be redeemed whereas man can be redeemed. The angels can only stand and peer down on the Mercy Seat in wonder and awe.

The writer of the book of Hebrews used the Jewish tradition, in translating Psalm 8:4-8, to make a point about the humanity of Christ. He had already stated that Christ is higher (or "better") than the angels (Hebrew 1:1-14). But now he needs to show that Jesus, in His humanity, could die and had to die as the sacrifice for sin, to redeem man. Therefore, Christ was made a little lower than the angels for the brief period of His humanity so that He could die and complete the redemption process. When that process was completed He again became superior to the angels in every sense.

So it is with man: in his unregenerate state he is under the curse of sin; he has to die because of his sin. If man can die, then he is truly a little lower than God, and for this period he would also be a little lower than angels, since angels are eternal and cannot die. He is a little lower than God because the image of God is marred in him by sin. In his regenerated state the curse of sin is removed, and therefore, he is higher than the angels because Christ has restored the perfect image of God in him in the redemption, process. It is true that the physical body must still die or be changed into the glorified body. Christ, in the Resurrection, will bring with Him His redeemed who have died physically and give them their glorified body. Then the redeemed that are still alive at His appearing will have their physical body changed into the glorified body (see I Corinthians 15:50-53).

He made man higher than the animals of His creation because no animal is as beautifully made as man, nor is any animal a match for man as companion and friend:

> And the LORD God said, 'It is not good for the

man to be alone; I will make a companion for him. And out of the ground the LORD God formed every beast of the field, and every fowl of the air; and brought them to Adam to see what he would call them: and whatever Adam called each living creature, became its name. And Adam gave names to all cattle, and to the fowl of the air, and to every beast of the field; but there was not found among them a suitable companion for Adam. And so the LORD God caused a deep sleep to fall upon Adam, and while he slept God removed one of his ribs, and closed up the flesh in its place. And the rib, which the LORD God took from man, He used to create a woman, whom He then gave to the man. And Adam said, "This is now bone of my bones, and flesh of my flesh: she shall be called Woman, because she was taken from my body. Therefore a man shall leave his father and his mother, and shall be joined with his wife: and they shall become one body" (Genesis 2:18-24).

Animals, are not suitable companions for man because they do not have the mental process with which God created man. There is no animal with the power of "reasoned speech." There is also the eternity of the soul of man, which no animal can lay claim to; this also keeps it from being a true companion for man. Also, man had to have a companion that was suitable to mate with and produce offspring to populate the world. Therefore no other creature but a woman can be a suitable wife for a man.

Because man was created in the image of God, he was given authority over all God's creation: "And God blessed them, and God said to them, 'Be fruitful, and multiply, and replenish the earth, and subdue it: and have dominion over the fish of the sea, and over the fowl of the air, and over every living thing that moves upon the earth'" (Genesis 1:28). In this sense God placed man as a god over His creation. Man is the image or reflection of God to His creation.

To murder a man would be to strike out at God. For murder is a clear statement that God has made an improper judgment in creating man in His own image. The murderer is saying that the man whose life he takes is not worthy to bear the image of God. He is saying that the one he murders is wrong for such responsibility. The murderer is setting himself above God by his actions.

Murder is also striking out against God's authority. The murderer is saying that God is not Lord. His dreadful act takes away God's right to use the murdered man to help control creation.

Since man is created in the image of God the act of murder is a slap at God Himself. This is the essence of rebellion against God.

## (Man Was Created For God)

One great blessing on mankind is that God created man to worship, serve and fellowship with his Creator. John the apostle said it this way: "You can be sure that our fellowship is with the Father, and with his Son Jesus Christ" (I John 1:3).

Within the framework of God's purpose for man is included the idea of his "walking" with God. This is illustrated by the life of Enoch who was so faithful in his walk with God that he did not have to die; God translated him body and soul to be with Him:

> And Enoch was sixty-five years old, when his son Methuselah was born. And Enoch walked with God after the birth of Methuselah for three hundred years, and he had other sons and daughters. And Enoch lived a total of three hundred sixty-five years. And Enoch walked with God: and he was not seen any more for God took him (Genesis 5:21-24).

Likewise, Noah was so faithful in his walk with God that he and his family were saved, alone of all mankind, when God destroyed the rest of the human inhabitants of the earth:

> Noah was the only righteous man and the only one without fault in his generation, because he walked with God...And God said to Noah, "It is time for Me to destroy all life on earth, because the earth has been made totally evil by man; and therefore, I will destroy man with the earth...But with you I will establish My covenant" (Genesis 6:9, 13, 18).

The murderer would destroy this earthly fellowship of man with God. We saw this truth exhibited in our discussion of Cain's murder of Abel.

The same is true even when the slain is not walking in close communion with God. The potential for fellowship between an individual and God remains while there is life. The murderer destroys that potential when he takes the life of his victim. Our Lord's story of the Rich Man and Lazarus is a good example of death destroying the potential for fellowship between man and God: These two men died. The angels carried Lazarus to Abraham's bosom or paradise. The Rich Man awoke in torment. Seeing Lazarus in paradise the Rich Man asked Abraham to send him with a little water to cool his tongue. To which Abraham replied:

> Son, remember that your whole life has been blessed with good things, but Lazarus has only had evil things: but now he is comforted, and you are tormented. And beside all this, a great gulf exists between you and us: so that they, who would go from here to you, cannot, neither can they come to us, who would go from there (Luke 16:25-26)

In Deuteronomy 6:13, it is recorded, "You shall fear the Lord your God, and serve only Him, and you shall vow only by His name." The whole intent of man's life is service for God. God made us to be stewards of all the earth (Genesis 1:28). He also made us to be witnesses of His salvation (Matthew 28:19-20). The murderer cuts short this service to God. The murder of Stephen by the Jews is one instance of murder destroying the service of a man for God:

> When they heard these things, they were enraged, and they snarled at him showing their teeth in their anger. But he, being full of the Holy Spirit, looked up intently toward heaven, and saw the glory of God, and Jesus standing on the right hand of God, and said, "Look, I see heaven opened, and the Son of man is standing at the right hand of God." Then they screamed at him in rage, and covered their ears, and together they rushed at him, dragged him out of the city, and began to stone him. The witnesses laid down their coats at a young man's feet, whose name was Saul, so they could cast the first stones. And while they were stoning him Stephen, knelt and began to pray to God, saying, Lord Jesus, receive my spirit. And he cried with a loud voice, "Lord, do not charge this sin to them." And when he said this, he fell asleep (Acts 7:54-60).

## (Time For Man To Be Redeemed)

After the fall of man into sin, life became a time for man to repent of sin and be saved. The Lord states this idea in the second chapter of Revelation:

> In spite of this I have a few things against you, because you allowed that woman, that Jezebel, who calls herself a prophetess, to teach and to seduce my servants to be sexually immoral, and to eat things sacrificed to idols. And I gave her time to repent of her idolatry and

sexual immorality, and still she did not repent (vv.20-21).

God wants all men to repent and be saved. The best and worst; the richest and poorest; the ignorant and learned; young and old, they are all the same to God. He loves them all.

God is patient with sinful man. He gives him every opportunity to be saved, by pleading with him long and hard, and calling to man at every turn. He gives him a lifetime to turn from sin unto salvation.

The murderer, on the other hand, cuts his victim's time short, perhaps taking away the last opportunity for salvation.

God has commanded: "You shall not murder." Therefore the murderer has brought death to himself. It is not the judge or jury; it not the executioner; it is certainly not God. Man has his life in his own hands. Man as a would-be murderer or as a lost sinner can choose death for himself. The murderer does this by taking the life of another man; the lost sinner does this by rejecting Jesus Christ as Savior and Lord.

# Chapter 8

## Sexual Purity

(Exodus 20:14)
"You shall not commit adultery."

### - Introduction -

At one time it was taboo to speak openly about sex. It was not considered the topic of polite, genteel company. Many thought of it as a fit subject only for the gutter group. Never was it to be mentioned in mixed company: For such to be done was considered the height of poor taste and the depth of low morals. Parents were embarrassed to talk to their children about sex. This was something that was whispered about. They were "forever" going to talk to sister or brother about the birds and the bees; mostly that "forever" never came. So, sister learned about sex from her girl friends that were as poorly informed as she was, or worse she was educated by a boy friend to the permanent damage of character and life. Brother had no better options. His buddies were usually his main source of information. Like their female counterparts they were mostly harboring terrible misconceptions.

I suppose I shall never forget some of the grossly distorted ideas about the female anatomy that I heard as a young boy. Looking back on those tales it seems impossible that I could have believed some of the nonsense that I heard, but I know that I did accept some as fact; at least I wondered if the tales were true.

When parents did teach this subject to their children, more often than not, they taught it as something less than pure. Surely this was done because of misinformation accepted as truth by many parents. Other parents may have taught their children that sex was evil with the thought that it might keep their children from experimenting in that area. Whatever the reason, it is a sad teaching that is completely untrue to the Bible.

The schools were not allowed to teach about sex. Most parents were frightened by the thought that their child would be filled with desire more than knowledge. Many mothers and fathers were even surer that their children would learn the wrong information from ill-informed teachers. Perhaps, they were afraid that their children might learn more than they knew.

Whatever the reason, the schools were restricted from teaching this subject for many years.

Numbers of girls have gone into marriage with a warped concept of the sexual relationship between husband and wife. This is true because their mothers had taught them, by word or action, that it was a necessary evil to be avoided as much as possible. This reminds me of what Christ said of the Pharisees as teachers: "If the blind lead the blind, both will fall into the ditch" (Matthew 15:14).

As a result of the forgoing we have been passing through a sexual revolution. Children found out that their parents, many times, were wrong in their ideas concerning sex, in and out of marriage. So they decided to take the matter into their own hands and deal with it as they saw fit. They could do no worse than their parents had done, or so they thought.

What has the sexual revolution gained for our world? We are seeing sex abused as much or more than ever before. Those who would do better than their parents generally find themselves making their own blunders and mistakes that cause as much pain and heartache as the errors of those who preceded them. Now sex is blatantly discussed with a freedom that exceeds the bounds of good taste or good sense. Overindulgence in anything can bring on problems. Too much freedom in this area of open discussion usually results in too much freedom in actions, which results in sexual promiscuity. Sexual promiscuity, more often than not, results in broken health, lives and homes.

Parents are often still shirking their responsibility this matter. They still do not talk as openly and clearly as they ought with their children. So for all the sexual revolution and freedom, we are still at square one in the proper dissemination of information concerning this most abused subject.

In some instances, the subject is being mishandled in the schools. This is often due to poorly qualified teachers. In other cases it is due to the poor morals of some teachers. Then again others are mishandling it in the name of fairness. Such is the case when it is taught that homosexuality is an acceptable alternate lifestyle or, when high school and junior high school boys and girls are taught that the real problem with premarital sex is getting pregnant, or being exposed to sexually transmitted diseases. So they are taught about the need for condoms and contraceptives. What such teaching really is, is sin. Such teaching is contrary to God's Word.

We need to go back to the Bible for a proper understanding of this subject. God plainly teaches in His Word: "You shall not commit adultery." Therefore He is calling for Sexual Purity in His creation.

## - Sexual Purity Before Marriage -

This Commandment speaks of much more than marriage fidelity; Jesus interpreted it to include the meaning of the broader term fornication:

> You have heard that it was said to them in times past, 'You shall not commit adultery:' But I say to you, 'That whoever looks at a woman and desires to have her sexually has already committed adultery with her in his heart'...'Whoever divorces his wife, except for sexual misconduct on her part, makes an adulteress of her: and whoever marries her that is divorced commits adultery' (Matthew 5:27-28, 32).

The dictionary defines adultery as the "Violation of the marriage bed; sexual intercourse between a married man and a woman not his wife, or between a married woman and a man not her husband."

The dictionary defines fornication as "voluntary sexual intercourse between an unmarried woman and man, especially an unmarried man. If the man or woman is married then it is adultery."

So, since Jesus interpreted this Commandment in the broader term fornication it speaks to the single as well as the married. This is true because our Lord is saying that this Commandment refers to lustful thoughts regardless of whether an illicit sexual act is performed. Actually He is telling us that to create and to live out, within the mind, illicit sexual fantasies is sin. He is also teaching that sex outside the marriage covenant is sin, regardless of whether the parties are married or single: "Marriage is honorable for all, and the marital bed should be kept pure: but God will judge the sexually immoral persons and adulterers" (Hebrews 13:4).

There is much talk today about free love, or freedom of sexual love without the bonds of marriage and without the responsibility of marriage. God says it is sin: "You shall not commit adultery."

How free is such love? Sin is never free. It always charges and collects a fee. The writer of Proverbs said, "Whoever commits adultery with a woman does not understand, that if he does this he will destroy his own soul" (Proverbs 6:32). It costs a soiled reputation, a spoiled body, or very possibly a diseased body, or a child without a complete name or a complete home. It can also cost the loss of a complete education and a forced marriage. Such costs are terribly high prices to pay for a moment of physical pleasure. To say the least, the writer of the book of Proverbs certainly knew what he talking about, and we find the same truth taught all the way through God's Book.

Ruben, the eldest son of Jacob, committed adultery with Bilhah the concubine of Jacob (Genesis 35:22). This resulted in a breach between father and son that was never healed.

On his deathbed Jacob called this sin of Reuben's into account:

> Reuben, you are my firstborn, my power, and the beginning of my strength, the first in position, and the strongest of all: But because you are as unruly as waves of the sea, you shall no longer be first in rank; because you went and defiled your father's bed; you dishonored me with one of my wives" (Genesis 49:3-4).

Reuben's sin is also called into account when the Law was given: "Cursed is he that has sex with his father's wife" (Deuteronomy 27:20). He also paid the penalty in the loss of his birthright:

> Now the sons of Reuben the oldest son of Israel lost their birthright, (for he was the firstborn; but because he dishonored me with one of my wives, his birthright was given to the sons of Joseph the son of Israel: therefore Reuben is not listed in the genealogy as the firstborn son. The children of Judah became the strongest tribe ruling over the other tribes, and descending from him came the chief ruler; but the status of being first born went to the children of Joseph) (I Chronicles 5:1-2).

Samson's affair with Delilah resulted in his capture by the Philistines, his eyes gouged out (the Hebrew word used here was "na'qar", pronounced "*naw-kar'* " is literally translated "dig, pick out, pierce, put (thrust) out"). He was then made to pull the millstone, for his enemies, like a beast of burden. Then he died with his enemies when he destroyed the pagan temple of Dagon, the Philistine god (Judges 16:4-30).

The destructiveness of fornication is clearly seen in the story of the incestuous rape of King David's daughter Tamar by her half brother Amnon. A young woman's chastity was violated, a murder was committed and a father lost two sons (II Samuel 13:1-39). That is a sad commentary on sex outside the sanctity of marriage.

The apostle Paul, writing under the inspiration of the Holy Spirit has much to say concerning the evils of fornication:

> It is reported that fornication is common among you, and that fornication that you are guilty of is such that is not even practice by the Gentiles: that one should have his father's wife. And you are proud of the deed, rather than mourning because he that has done this has not been removed from your fellowship. For I truly, though absent in body, but present in spirit, have already

judged, as though I were present, concerning him who has done this deed. In the name of our Lord Jesus Christ, when you are gathered together, with my spirit, and with the power of our Lord Jesus Christ, deliver such a person to Satan for the destruction of the flesh, that the spirit may be saved in the day of the Lord Jesus...I wrote to you in an epistle not to have fellowship with fornicators: however we are not speaking of the fornicators of this world, or with the covetous, or swindlers, or with idolaters; for to do so would require you to leave this world. But now I have written to you that you should not have fellowship with any man that is called a Christian who is a fornicator, or who is covetous, or who is an idolater, or who is a crude person, or who is a drunkard, or who is a swindler. You should not even eat with such persons. For what right do I have to judge them who are outside the fellowship? But are we not supposed to judge those who are within the fellowship? But those who are outside the fellowship God will judge. Therefore remove that wicked person from your fellowship (I Corinthians 5:1-5, 9-13).

In the foregoing passage Paul makes it clear that fornication is not to be tolerated in the membership of the church. It is unchristian and damaging to the fellowship. It is to be dealt with immediately for the good of all concerned. Then he adds an explicit judgment on such unrighteousness:

Do you not know the unrighteous will not inherit the kingdom of God? Do not be deceived no fornicator, idolater, adulterer, homosexual, or sodomite or thief, or covetous person, or drunkard, or abusive person, or swindler will inherit the kingdom of God (I Corinthians 6:9-10).

Notice the company kept by the fornicator in Paul's judgment: idol worshipers, adulterers, effeminates (boys used by sodomites, or the male who plays the role of the female in the homosexual relationship) and abusers of themselves with mankind (Greek "arsenokoites" which is translated a sodomite or homosexual).

For those who think that only the Old Testament teaches against homosexuality, this is only one verse of many in the New Testament that teach likewise (see Romans 1:24, 26, 27; I 1:9-10). The Word plainly says that those who practice such things, as a way of life, will not be a part of God's Kingdom. They are all sins of immorality and will not be tolerated by God.

Paul strengthens his argument in the following verses:

> Don't you know that your bodies are joined to Christ? Shall I then take the body of Christ, and join it to an immoral woman? God forbid. What? Don't you know that he that is joined to an immoral woman becomes one body with her? For two, says the Lord, shall be one flesh. But he that is joined to the Lord is one spirit. Run away fornication. Every other sin that a man does is outside the body; but he that commits fornication sins against his own body. What? Don't you know that your body is the temple of the Holy Spirit who dwells in you, who was given to you by God, and you are not your own? For you are bought with a price: therefore glorify God in your body, and in your spirit, which are God's (I Corinthians 6:15-20).

To the great apostle Paul it is the ultimate sin for the Christian to participate in physical immorality, for it desecrates the body, which is the abode of Christ's Spirit, and therefore makes the Lord a part of the evil deed.

Several years ago there was a popular song, entitled "Love and Marriage," that is most applicable to this subject. The song says, "Love and marriage, love and marriage they go together like a horse and carriage. Dad was told by mother 'You can't have one without the other.'"

It takes very little common sense to understand that "love and marriage" go together. Within the bonds of matrimony there is the home to nurture the love of husband and wife. There also is the God-given place to rear children. All other unions are not blessed or prospered; they only bring pain. All other unions are immoral and abnormal in the sight of God.

God has said so plainly, "You shall not commit adultery," that there is no question that He demands a knowledge and observance of:

## - Sexual Purity In Marriage -

Marriage, love, and sex are important necessities of this life. God made it so.

> So God created man in his own image, in the image of God He created him, male and female He created them. And God blessed them, and God said to them, "Be fruitful, and multiply, and replenish the earth, and bring it under your control: have power over the fish of the

sea, and over the fowl of the air, and over every living
thing that moves on the earth (Genesis 1:27-28).

The foregoing Scripture says man and woman were created to populate the earth. Since this was before the fall of man, it is fair to say that sex was not the sin that caused the fall. It is also obvious that God created the pair with procreation in mind: that is why He made them male and female, not male and male or female and female. It is also plain to see that Man and Woman were made to be partners in this estate in which the Creator placed them. In Genesis 2:21-23 we are given the details of woman's creation. From that account Charles Wesley wrote a hymn that says:

> Not from his head the woman took,
> And made her husband to overlook.
> Not from his feet, as one designed,
> The footstool of the stronger kind.
> But fashioned for himself a bride:
> An equal taken from his side.

I believe that because of this God said:

> For this reason a man shall leave his father and his
> mother, and shall be joined to his wife: and they shall
> become one body. (Genesis 2:24).

The two are to be one in every sense of the word. It is to be as the marriage vows say, "One in thought, intent and hope in all the interests of this present life."

It is for these reasons that we believe that sex in marriage is holy. God told Eve, "Your desire *shall* be to your husband" (Genesis 3:16). The writer of the book of Hebrews states it in this way, "Marriage is honorable for all, and the marital bed should be kept pure: but God will judge the sexually immoral persons and adulterers" (Hebrews 13:4). Only the evil, debased, or terribly uninformed mind will make the physical relationship between husband and wife sordid, shameful, and sinful.

It is also true that God intended sex in marriage to be a blessing. Sex is the expression of love and concern between man and wife, not just animal lust. In marriage sex has a blessed purpose: The creation of a new life that makes the husband and wife one flesh in reality. Paul says marriage is a necessity for most men and women: "To avoid fornication let every man have his own wife, and let every woman have her own husband" (I Corinthians 7:2). He adds, "it is better to marry than to burn" with sexual desire and have no sacred means to fulfill that desire (I Corinthians 7:9).

God says that infidelity in marriage is evil, and destructive:

> The lips of an immoral woman drip with the
> sweetness of a honeycomb, and her words are smoother

than oil. (Proverbs 5:3).

Sometimes old relationships become unresponsive and unfulfilling through indifference created by taking one's mate, or one's marriage bed for granted. It is true that at such times there may be physical pleasure found for the moment in a sexual relationship with a new partner: It may seem as sweet as honey, however, the sin that is involved is terribly destructive and the pain caused by that sin is forever.

The writer of Proverbs follows with his answer concerning this situation: "The after results are as bitter as gall and the conscience is constantly wounded by the infidelity" (Proverbs 5:3-4). To increase the strength of his argument the Solomon says:

> Can a man take fire in his arms and hold it to his breast, and his clothes not be burned? Can one walk on hot coals, and his feet not be burned? So is the result to the one who commits adultery with his neighbor's wife: whoever sexually embraces her, will be punished (Proverbs 6:27-29).

Adultery is never acceptable except to a debased mind and heart. It always brings heartache, pain and the condemnation of conscience. Abraham's pain over Ishmael testifies that his relationship with Hagar was wrong (Genesis 17:18; 21:9-11). Everyone in that situation was damaged. Abraham's wife Sarah was held in contempt by her handmaid, Hagar (Genesis 16:4). Hagar and Ishmael felt the full impact of this situation when Abraham had to send them away (Genesis 21:14-21). Also, there has never been any peaceful relationship between the descendants of Isaac, the son of Abraham and Sarah, and the descendants of Ishmael, the son of the handmaid. I doubt if Sarah ever forgave Abraham for this plight even though she was the instigator of the situation that caused the difficulties.

We discussed David's adulterous affair with Bathsheba in Chapter Seven. However, there was one painful occurrence that we did not mention. The child that was born of their sin became terribly ill. David fasted and prayed for seven days and nights for God to spare the child, but the child died (II Samuel 12:15- 23). The short life of that baby was a constant reminder of the parents' sin.

A most pointed incident, as to the results of the evils of adultery, is found in I Samuel 2:22-25:

> Now Eli was very old when he heard what his sons were doing to all the people of Israel. He was aware that they were seducing the women who were helping at the entrance of the tabernacle of the congregation. So, he said to them, "Why are you doing such things? All the

people have told me of your evil dealings. No, my sons, it is not a good report that I have heard. You are causing the Lord's people to sin. If a man sins against another man, the judge will judge him: but if a man sin against the Lord, who will be there to intercede for him?" However they did not listen to the pleas of their father, because the Lord was already planning to put them to death.

Here the priests of God profaned the house of the Lord and did terrible harm to the cause of God. They took advantage of the women who came to worship at the door of the tabernacle. Using their position as religious leaders, they committed adultery. It never fails that when men of God sin the harm is devastating. It does not matter that they are men subject to the same passions as are all men. They are expected to live exemplary lives. They certainly pay the same price if not a higher price than other men when they sin. In this particular case the Lord did kill them by the hand of the Philistine army:

> And the Philistines fought valiantly, and Israel was routed before them, and the men of Israel fled to their tents: and there were a great many who were slaughtered: thirty thousand soldiers died in that battle. The Philistines confiscated the ark of God, and killed Eli's two sons, Hophni and Phinehas (I Samuel 4:10-11).

It matters not whether it is preacher or layman, adultery is unacceptable to God, and He will punish the offender. Again God said, "You shall not commit adultery." This Commandment demands a knowledge and observance of:

## - Sexual Purity In Divorce -

Divorce has come down on our present world like a plague. Jesus agreed with this when He said:

> Have you not read, that He who, in the beginning, created all things made them male and female, and said, "For this cause a man shall leave father and mother, and shall merge with his wife, and they who had been two shall be one body:" The result is that they are no more two, but one body. Therefore those, whom God has merged into one body, let no man separate (Matthew 19:4-6).

God did not intend for there to be divorce. So men today, like the

Pharisees of Jesus' day, ask "Why then did Moses command that a certificate of divorce be written, for a man to be able to divorce his wife?" (Matthew 19:7).

I once knew a woman who practiced this. She asked my wife to pickup a layaway from a local store for her. When my wife went to the store and to get the layaway, and gave the clerk the name she knew the woman by. After some time the clerk returned and said there was no layaway in that name. My wife called the woman and told her the problem. To which she answered, "Maybe I put it in one of my other names." My wife then gave the clerk the other names and the layaway was found. Later, when we questioned her about the use of the other names she explained: "I have been married several times." To which I asked, "Oh, you have been divorced?" She said, "Yes. I did what the Bible said to do: I wrote out a certificate of divorce and put it in their hand." She had never been through the courts, yet she was perfectly satisfied. But Jesus' answer to this was: "Moses allowed you to divorce your wives because of the hardness of your hearts, but God, from the beginning, did not intend this to be" (Matthew 19:8).

Jesus mentions only two types of divorce that are approved in heaven:

> And I tell you, whoever divorces his wife, and then marry another, unless she has committed fornication, commits adultery. And whoever marries her who is divorced commits adultery (Matthew 19:9).

The first type of divorce, mentioned here by implication, is legal separation. That is divorce from living together, but not from the bonds of marriage. This is also taught by Paul in I Corinthians 7:10-11:

> And to the married I command, or rather the Lord commands, "Do not permit the wife to leave her husband. However if she insists on leaving, let her remain unmarried, or else be reconciled to her husband, and the husband must not divorce her.

The second type is divorce because of infidelity by the husband or wife. Here the husband or wife who sinned is the same as dead to their partner.

In I Corinthians 7:12-17 Paul adds another reason for divorce that frees the parties to remarry that is not stated by our Lord:

> But to the rest I speak, not the Lord: If any brother has a wife who is not a believer, and she is satisfied to live with him, he must not divorce her. And the woman who has a husband who does not believe, and if he is

satisfied to live with her, she should not divorce him. For the wife sanctifies the unbelieving husband, and the husband sanctifies the unbelieving wife: or else their children would be unclean; but now are they holy. But if the unbelieving mate leaves, let him go. A brother or a sister is not bound in such a situation: but God has called us to live in peace. For what makes you thank, O wife, if you will be able to lead you husband to be saved? Or what makes you believe, O man, whether you will lead your wife to salvation? But as God has given to every man, as the Lord has called every one, so let him walk. And so I decreed in all the churches

I know that many will disagree with me at this point, but Paul plainly say, "A brother or a sister is not under bondage in such situations" (v. 15). It was the lost partner's decision to leave; therefore they have broken the bonds of marriage. They bear the responsibility for their unfaithfulness to the marriage. This is the infidelity that frees the Christian mate from the bonds of marriage and allows them to remarry without bearing the charge of adultery. Divorce for any other reason makes remarriage adultery.

The Mosaic law of divorce adds one thing Christ or Paul does not mention: If a man divorces his wife, and she marries another, and then she is divorced again, her first husband may not remarry her (Deuteronomy 24:1-4).

This question of divorce and remarriage is a difficult one, but I believe that the above covers the Biblical answers as thoughtfully and completely as man can arrive at an answer. We certainly need to exercise caution at this point in the marriage relationship. Divorce should never be the easy or the first answer to difficulties in a marriage.

God has plainly said, "Thou shall not commit adultery." Shall we not understand this command to be a call for man to be morally pure as directed by God's Holy Word, and not according to the lust of the flesh? We must if we are to ever be acceptable to our Creator and Lord.

# Chapter 9

## God's Call For Honesty

(Exodus 20:15)
"You shall not steal"

### - Introduction -

There does not seem to be anything that men will not steal. Several years ago I read a newspaper article, entitled "Somebody's Stealing A Bridge." The item went on to say, "A bridge rustler is on the loose in Traverse City, Michigan. Eleven three-foot-wide steel I-beams, each fifteen feet long were stolen from a bridge construction site." That was certainly no small undertaking. The sheer weight of the beams would require a tremendous amount of power to lift, not to mention the difficulty in hauling them away. There had to be some powerful motivation behind the theft, not only to make the effort worthwhile, but also to make taking such a risk profitable. To be sure selfishness lay at the root of the motive. They surely thought the return would be worth the effort and danger involved in the theft. God says that this should not be so: "You shall not steal."

There are three things found in this Commandment: The wellspring from which stealing arises; a demand for honesty between men; a call for honesty from man to God. First, to understand God's call for honesty, we need knowledge of:

### - The Primary Source Of All Stealing -

The primary source of all stealing is a bad heart. This truth is testified to in both the Old Testament and the New Testament. The prophet Jeremiah stated it this way: "The heart *is* deceitful above all *things*, and desperately wicked: who can understand it?" (Jeremiah 17:9). Simply, he is saying that the wellspring of evil is within man, not from some exterior source.

We cannot blame God for our waywardness and corruption. Nor can we place the fault with our parents. Our fellowman is not responsible for the evil that we do. Even though Satan is the tempter and destroyer, we cannot lay our problem at his doorstep. Jesus echoed this same thought when He said:

> Either make the tree good, and its fruit good; or else make the tree corrupt, and its fruit corrupt: for the tree is known by the fruit it bears. You generation of vipers, how can you, being evil, speak good things? For from the many things found in the heart the mouth speaks A good man out of the good treasure of the heart brings out good things: and an evil man out of the evil treasure brings out evil things (Matthew 12:33-35).

It is not just evil deeds that come from the heart of man, but wicked speech also finds its origin there. The story is told of a little boy who constantly used vulgar language. One day a man heard him and asked, "Who pays you to use such profanity and vulgarity?" The boy quickly replied, "No one, mister." The man's response was, "You certainly do work cheap for the disgrace you bring on your mother and father, your good name, and the damning of your eternal soul!"

If man is innately good, as some like to think and teach, then why in all the history of man has he not been able to improve his life and conduct? It is because man is inherently wicked. He has a bad heart. That is the source of all sin, including stealing.

Again, we find the truth of this in the words of our Master. He places the blame squarely on the shoulders of man himself. According to our Lord every evil act committed by man finds its conception in man's inward being, including stealing. James, the half brother of Jesus, also has a pertinent word in this matter:

> But every man is tempted, when he is enticed and drawn away by his own lust. Then when lust has conceived, it produces sin: and sin, when it is finished, results in death (James 1:14-15).

All sin finds its inception in man's lust of mind, soul and body. The wickedness of man is in the selfish desires formed in his innermost being. So, the thief is responsible for his stealing and no one else.

This waywardness of man does not come from ignorance. God has instructed man in the way he should walk:

> But this thing I commanded them, saying, "Obey my voice and I will be your God, and you shall be my people: and walk in all the ways that I have commanded you, so that it may be well with you" (Jeremiah 7:23).

So God has issued the commandments to man, which includes this present commandment: "You shall not steal." He is saying, "I have not left you without knowledge of the Way. I have given you My Commandments, I sent My Son Jesus to show you the way of obedience and He has sent Our

Holy Spirit to guide you in that way. Now you are without excuse." But man has not listened to the voice of God. Instead he has listened to the commands of his own evil heart. What God said of His people Israel He also says to those who violate His Commandments today:

> But they did not listen, nor turn their ear, but walked in the counsels and the imagination of their evil heart, and went backward, and not forward...Therefore, behold, the days come, says the Lord, that...the dead bodies of these people shall be meat for the fowls of the heaven, and for the beasts of the earth; and none shall drive them away. Then will I cause the voice of mirth, and the voice of gladness, the voice of the bridegroom, and the voice of the bride to cease in the cities of Judah, and in the streets of Jerusalem,: for the land shall be desolate (Jeremiah 7:24, 32-34).

Israel lost the blessings of God for not listening to His warnings; instead they listened to the evil counsel of their own hearts. So all the failures and losses that man suffers arise from his own wickedness and waywardness, which come of his disobedience to God's Law. This is true because man prefers his own counsel rather than the warnings of God.

In Proverbs 27:19, we read, "As in water a face reflects its self, so the heart of man reflects who he really is." If you want to know and understand a man then look inside his heart. His heart reflects what he is, just as his face is reflected in a pool of water.

Will a study of men's actions bear out the above? Let us look at the lives of some individuals and see if their actions do exhibit what the Word of God has said: The source of all the evil acts of man, including stealing, is found within man himself:

Jacob cheated his brother Esau out of his birthright (Genesis 25:29-34). Even though Esau despised his birthright and sold it for a bowl of stew, it does not relieve Jacob of his sin. Jacob took advantage of Esau's weakness and drove a hard bargain to get the birthright, and that is stealing. Then Jacob and his mother, Rebekah conspired together to steal Esau's blessing (Genesis 27:1-41). The record is plain concerning these deeds. To read them is to see that these thefts came directly from the hearts of Jacob and Rebekah. They chose to do the evil deeds freely and deliberately. No outside cause is found, only their own evil desires caused their sin.

## - Secondary Sources For Stealing -

### (Extreme poverty)

Victor Hugo's "Les Miserables" is a masterpiece of literature about how extreme poverty can lead to stealing. Jean Valjean, the hero of the novel, steals bread to feed his starving family and himself. He spends nineteen years in prison for his crime. One cannot help but feel pity for this man. The Bible says that this sympathy is normal to man: "Men do not despise a thief, if he steal to satisfy his soul when he is hungry" (Proverbs 6:30). However, it goes on to say, "But if he is found out, he shall restore seven times as much as he stole; he shall give all the possessions found in his house"(Proverbs 6:31). Hunger cannot justify stealing. Only a bad heart justifies its own evil deeds.

## (Laziness)

The writer of Proverbs points out the evils and sorrow of the lazy person:

> I went by the field of the lazy man, by the vineyard of the man without understanding; and, I saw that it was overgrown with thorns. Nettles had covered the ground, and its stonewall was broken down. Then I thought about what I saw, and I learned a lesson: A little too much sleep, a little more slumber, a little folding of the hands to rest, and poverty will come on you like a bandit, and your needs will attack you like an armed thief (Proverbs 24:30-34).

The lazy individual will not turn his hand to an honest living. If he does accept a job from someone, he will do as little as is possible. He will take the wages, but he will not return an honest days work for that pay. That is stealing just as surely as if that lazy employee had opened the employer's wallet and stolen the money.

## (Living Beyond One's Means)

The Lord tells a parable, in Luke 16:1-7, of a servant who was wasteful with his master's property. The servant was told that he was to be audited. To which he thought, "What can I do? For my lord is going to take the stewardship away from me. I cannot dig; to I am too proud to beg" (v. 3). He was used to living in his employer's house and being cared for by his employer. To lose this was more than the man could stand. The thought of giving up what he had was intolerable. So he decided to steal from his master. How many persons have embezzled from their employer to keep from giving up their way of life? God says, "You shall not steal, deal falsely, nor lie one to another" (Leviticus 19:11).

## (A Love Of Ostentation)

Amos was a stern prophet. He had little tolerance for the rich and powerful of Samaria. He called the first ladies of the town "cows," "drunks" and "gluttons." He warned them that they had better enjoy their ill-gotten gain while they could. It was not because they were rich that he despised them and spoke so roughly to them, but it was how they got their riches that troubled him. He knew that it was by stealing from the poor:

> Hear this word, you cows of Bashan, that live in the mountain of Samaria, who oppress the poor, who crush the needy, who say to their husbands, "Bring wine, and let us drink"...A woe is pronounced on them who are at ease in Zion, and trust in the mountain of Samaria, who are called chief of the nations, to whom the house of Israel came...You who refuse to think about the evil you are storing up for yourselves, and the resulting judgment that is coming on you...That lie upon ivory beds, and stretch yourselves on your couches, and eat the lambs out of the flock, and the calves out of the of the stall; That chant to the sound of the viol, *and* invent to yourselves instruments of music, like David; That drink wine from bowls, and anoint yourselves with precious ointments: but who do not care that your nation is going to ruin. (Amos 4:1; 6:1, 4-6).

He went on to pronounce God's judgment on them for their corruption:

> The Lord God has sworn by His holiness, that, lo, the days shall come upon you, that He will lead you away with hooks, and your children with fishhooks... Therefore you shall be the first who go into captivity; then your celebrating will end (Amos 4:2; 6:7).

## (The love of money)

Paul in cautioning the young preacher, Timothy, against allowing himself to be ensnared by possessions said,

> But godliness with contentment is a very profitable place to be. For we brought nothing into *this* world, *and it is* certain we can carry nothing out. So let us be content with having sufficient food and clothing. But

those who desire to be rich are overcome by temptations, traps, and many foolish and harmful lusts, which drag men down into destruction and ruin. For the love of money is the root of all kinds of evil; which is what some have lusted after, erring from the faith, and piercing themselves through with much heartache. But you, O man of God, run from these things; and follow after righteousness, godliness, faith, love, patience, and meekness (I Timothy 6:6-11).

One example of how the love of money trapped a man and his family is found in the story of Achan, a member of the Israeli army that conquered Jericho, under the leadership of Joshua:

And Achan answered Joshua, and said, "It is true, I have sinned against the Lord God of Israel, and this is what I have done: When I saw among the spoils a beautiful Babylonian garment, and two hundred silver coins, and a bar of gold weighing more than a pound, I coveted them, and took them. Look for yourself, you will find these things buried in the sand under my tent, with the silver on the bottom" (Joshua 7:20-21).

The sad conclusion to this story is that Achan and his entire family died horrible deaths for his love of money (Joshua 7:24-25).

Unfortunately men called of God to be ministers are not immune to this evil. While at the home of Martha and Mary in Bethany, Mary anointed the feet of Jesus. Judas Iscariot was indignant over what she did, calling it a waste and saying that ointment should have been sold and the money given to the poor. John, in his gospel gave the real reason for Judas' objection: "He said this, not because he was concerned for the poor; but because he was a thief, and kept the funds for the group" (John 12:6).

Perhaps Paul was thinking of Judas Iscariot when he cautioned Timothy about the danger of the love of money.

### (A sick mind: Kleptomania)

Kleptomania is the only cause of stealing that is not mentioned in the Bible. Some people develop an aberration of the mind and go through life stealing. They apparently are unable to control the impulse that causes them to steal, and need seems to have no bearing what they steal.

I heard of a wealthy merchant in a certain town whose wife suffered from kleptomania. He went to all the other merchants in town and told them to keep track of what his wife stole from them and send him a bill and he would pay them.

The woman would steal items for which she had no need, and would then hide them away in closets for fear of being caught. Instead of living with and covering up her problem, she and her husband needed to locate a good Christian psychologist to help find a cure for her problem. The situation mentioned, however, happened many years ago, so perhaps the help needed was not available at that time.

I do not believe that God would want us to live with, or hide such a problem. Nor do I believe that He would want us to make excuses for stealing for any reason. Like those who came to Jesus with physical illnesses, I believe that we may take mental illnesses to Him also. If He has the power to cure the body He surely has the remedy for mental illness.

Next we find, in this Commandment, God's call for:

## - Honesty From Man To Man -

"You shall not steal" that which belongs to your fellow man: his personal property. Personal property can take many forms, and may include material, spiritual, physical, mental possessions, and personal rights. The open violation of this law includes robbery, burglary, theft, and kidnapping.

Jezebel's theft of Naboth's vineyard (I Kings 21:2-16) is a clear example of an evil heart being the cause of stealing, and also an accurate illustration of stealing a man's material possession, his reputation, and a personal right. King Ahab saw that Naboth's land joined his, and that it was a choice piece of property. He approached Naboth with an offer to buy the land, but Naboth refused. It was his inheritance. He simply would not sell it for any price.

Ahab must have been a terribly spoiled individual. He must have never before been told no, or refused anything. He went back to the palace, went to bed and refused to eat. When Jezebel found Ahab in this state, she told him to rise and eat and be happy. She assured him that she would get the vineyard for him.

That wicked queen used her husband Ahab's power as king and gave orders to the elders of Naboth's city to hire evil men to give false testimony against Naboth so he could be put to death. So the deed was done, and Naboth was killed. When word arrived at the palace, Jezebel told Ahab to go and take Naboth's vineyard. God sent Elijah to meet Ahab in the vineyard and say to him: "And you shall speak to him, saying, 'Thus says the LORD, "Have you killed, and also taken possession?" And you shall speak to him, saying, "Thus says the LORD, 'In the place where dogs licked the blood of Naboth shall dogs lick your blood, even yours'"'" (I Kings

21:19).

## (The Right To Own And Keep Land)

Man has a right to space, and that right can be stolen from him. The prophet Isaiah raised this issue and pronounced a judgment on those guilty of this type of stealing.

> Woe to those who join house to house, and add field to field until no land remains, and they are left alone in the earth! (Isaiah 5:8).

The prophet Elijah said to Ahab:

> Because you have sold yourself to work evil in the sight of the Lord, consider that He will bring evil on you, and will destroy your descendants...And of Jezebel the Lord also said, 'The dogs will eat Jezebel's flesh by the wall of Jezreel (I Kings 21:20-21, 23).

## (The Right To Fellowship With God)

The right to worship is a God given right that is to be enjoyed by all men. God also commands that men will worship Him (See chapter two). To take that right away, whether it is to work or for play it is stealing. Many employers have stolen this right by demanding their employees work on the Lord's Day, and made keeping the job depend on obedience to the demand. That is stealing the employee's right to worship.

## (The Right To Oneself)

The sons of Jacob hated their brother Joseph. First they plotted to kill him, but instead of adding murder to their sin they sold him into slavery in a foreign country (Genesis 37:1-36). They stole Joseph's right to himself, and their father's right to his son. Since their hatred found its roots in their jealous hearts their theft came from the evil within them.

Today the kidnapper will kidnap a baby, a husband, or a wife and hold that one for ransom. That is stealing twice. First the kidnapper stole the person's right to himself. Then he stole by taking the ransom.

## (The Right To Have A Family)

The right to family and domestic joy is a most precious possession. You can steal a man's wife, and you destroy his joy. This is what David did to Uriah (II Samuel 11:2-4).

You can alienate the affections of a child. I have seen people do this with nephews and nieces. They were not able to have children of their own so they alienated the affections of the children of their brother or sister. That is stealing.

## (The Right To Have A Good Name)

A good name is precious indeed. Solomon, the wisest of men, said, "A good name is rather to be desired than great riches and loving favor more than silver and gold" (Proverbs 22:1). He repeated this same idea in Ecclesiastes 7:1, "A good name is better than precious ointment." To take this way from a man is to steal one of his most precious possessions.

When Joseph arrived in Egypt he was sold to Potiphar, an officer of Pharaoh. Being blessed of God, Joseph advanced quickly in the service of his master. Potiphar put him in charge of all that he possessed. From that point on Potiphar prospered. Evidently Joseph was not only an intelligent young man, but also most handsome. It was only a short time until Potiphar's wife desired him sexually. She propositioned him, but he refused. There is an old saying that must have found its basis in this story: "Hell has no fury like a woman scorned." In her anger she slandered him. She accused him of trying to rape her (Genesis 39:14-18). She stole away his good name in a sentence and his freedom with a word (Genesis 39:19-20).

Jezebel had Naboth slandered and stole not only his property, but also his good name and his life (I Kings 21:9-14).

The Jews slandered Jesus. They called Him a drunkard, a glutton and a friend of sinners (Matthew 11:19). The last charge was true, thank God. He truly is the friend of sinners. If that were not true He would never have come to earth and given Himself to be our Savior. The first two charges were lies told to ruin His reputation. Their intention was to destroy Him.

The Bible is most explicit about the gossip:

> You shall not go up and down spreading tales among your people...(Leviticus 19:16). The wicked man sows strife: and a gossip separates the best of friends (Proverbs 16:28).
>
> He that goes about carrying tales reveals secrets: therefore stay away from the one who flatters with his lips (Proverbs 20:19).
>
> Where there is no wood, the fire goes out: so where no one carries tales there will be no strife. The same way charcoal is affected by burning coals, and wood by fire is the same way a contentious man causes

strife. The words of a gossip wound the innermost parts of a person (Proverbs 26:20-22).

Do not speak evil of one another, brothers and sisters. He who speaks evil of his brother, and judges his brother, speaks evil of the law, and judges the law: but if you judge the law, you are not obeying the law, but have become a judge (James 4:11).

Gossip spreads lies that steal away a man's good name. The one who spreads gossip is a thief. God says of him, "Whoever secretly slanders his neighbor, I will destroy" (Psalm 101:5).

## (The Right To Time)

You must not work a man so many hours of the day or week, that he has no time for himself or his family. To not allow for this is to steal a valuable asset from that man.

## (The Right To Work)

Man is entitled to the right to work. In their beginnings, labor unions did much for the workingman in the United States. Gone are the sweatshops of that existed in the early days of the last century. Many injustices in the workplace have been removed. However, when these forces for good step in and create a situation in which a man cannot work it is stealing from that man. Man is not only entitled to the right to work, but he is also entitled to a fair profit for his labor. To force a man to work for wages that are less than the labor and time expended is to steal from that man.

There are also the veiled violations of this law that need to be considered:

First we consider the merchant who has scales that weigh heavy. So, when he weighs merchandise it will always weigh more than the actual weight. When you sell by weight and do this, you are stealing. If you use a yardstick that is not thirty-six inches long, then you cheat on the merchandise being measured. That is stealing. The service station owner has his gas pumps set to display one price per gallon, but has set them to charge another price is also a thief. It is recorded in the Word of God: "You shall not have in your bag different weights, one heavy and one light" (Deuteronomy 25:13).

If you have an item that belongs to your neighbor and he comes for it and you tell him you do not have it today, but if he will come back tomorrow you will have it; then you are stealing from that neighbor: "Do not say to your neighbor, 'Go away for now, and come again tomorrow I will give you what you ask;' when you have it with you" (Proverbs 3:28).

How many times have you seen someone trying to bargain for an item and they begin by saying how bad it is? If it is an automobile it is dented and rusty, or the engine does not sound good. Then when they have bought it, they go and brag about what a bargain they got. This is exactly what Proverbs 20:14, says: "The buyer says 'It is bad, it is bad,' but when he is gone his way, then he boasts" That is stealing.

God says, "You shall not steal." This brings us to God's call for:

## - Honesty From Man To God -

"You shall not steal," that which belongs to God:

God has required that man reserve some things for Him and for Him alone. In the beginning He reserved one tree in the Garden of Eden for Himself, saying to Adam and Eve:

> "You may freely eat of every tree in the garden. But you shall not eat of the tree of the knowledge of good and evil. For in the day that you eat of it you will surely die." (Genesis 2:16-17).

That tree was set apart for God alone. Man was not to touch it.

### (The Tithes)

We find in Genesis 14:1-20, that Abraham understood this requirement. There we are told that the land was at war with the four kings of the north: Chedorlaomer, king of Elam; Amraphel, king of Babylon; Arioch, king of Ellasar; and Tidal, king of Goiim. Chedorlaomer, along with his allies, came to punish the five kings of the south: Bera, king of Sodom; Birsha, king of Gomorrah; Shinab, king of Admah; Shemeber, king of Zeboiim; and the king of Zoar for their rebellion against his rule over them.

For twelve years the five kings of the south had been subject to King Chedorlaomer, but now in the thirteenth year, they rebelled against him. They mobilized their armies in the valley of the Dead Sea and made ready for war. In the fourteenth year, Chedorlaomer and his allies arrived and the battle began.

The armies of the five kings of the south were unsuccessful in their war against the four kings of the north. Chedorlaomer and his allies plundered Sodom and Gomorrah and carried off all their people, including Abraham's nephew Lot and his family. Then the four kings headed back to their own land.

Now it happened that one of the men of Sodom had escaped and went and told Abraham, who was encamped among the oaks on the land that belonged to Mamre the Amorite.

When Abraham heard that Lot had been captured, he called together the 318 men born into his household. He asked his allies, Mamre and his brothers Eshcol and Aner, to join him in an attempt to rescue his nephew and family. They armed their men and went after the retiring army as far as Dan. There Abraham divided his men and made a night raid on the armies of the four kings. He recovered everything that had been taken, including his nephew Lot and all of Lot's family and possessions.

As Abraham was returning from his raid on Chedorlaomer and his allies, the king of Sodom, and Melchizedek, the king of Salem, who was a priest of God, came out to meet him. Then Melchizedek blessed Abraham saying "Blessed be Abram by God Most High, Creator of heaven and earth. And blessed be God Most High, who has helped you conquer your enemies" (Genesis 14:19-20). Then Abraham gave Melchizedek a tithe of all that he had taken in the raid on the four kings of the north.

Abraham's grandson Jacob learned and accepted the truth of God's requirement of the tithe in a most difficult way. He and his mother Rebekah had plotted and took his brother Esau's inheritance and birthright. When Esau realized what they had done he wanted to kill Jacob. So Rebekah, to save Jacob from Esau, had her husband Isaac send Jacob to her brother Laban in Padan Aram. So Jacob left home for the first time in his life and headed for his uncle Laban's home in Padan Aram.

Jacob was now alone in the desert when night fell. He took a rock for a pillow and lay down to sleep. As he slept he dreamed that he saw a golden ladder with one end resting on the earth and the other end reaching into heaven. Ascending and descending the ladder were the angels of God. Standing at the top God spoke to Jacob saying,

> I am the LORD God of your fathers Abraham, and Isaac. The land on which you lie, I will give to you, and to your descendants. And your descendants will be as numerous as the dust of the earth, and you will spread abroad to the west, and to the east, and to the north, and to the south: and you and your descendants shall bless all the families of the earth. And, consider this, I will be with you, and will protect you in every place you go, and I will bring you back to this land. For I will not leave you, until I have done what I have said I will do for you (Genesis 28:13-15).

I believe that Jacob was converted that night. God not only saved

Jacob, but also changed him from a self-centered manipulator into a generous, obedient servant who could now be useful to mankind.

The next morning, when Jacob awoke, he pledged to give God the tenth of his income from that time forward. Now God had not only the man, but also his pocketbook.

When the Law was given to Moses on Mt. Sinai, God included tithing as a part of the Law for God's people:

> And all the tithe of the land, whether of the seed of the land, or of the fruit of the tree, is the Lord's: it is set aside as holy for the Lord (Leviticus 27:30).

Jesus verified this truth in Matthew 23:23, saying, "Woe to you hypocritical, scribes and Pharisees! For you pay tithe of mint and anise and cummin, and have omitted the more important teachings of the law, judgment, mercy, and faith: these you should have done, and not left the other undone."

The apostle Paul taught the practice of tithing to the churches that he started on his mission trips: "On the first day of the week let every one of you set aside in store according to that which God has prospered you, so that there will be no collections taken when I come" (I Corinthians 16:2). Now, I know that Paul was speaking of the offering that was being taken for the poor of the Church in Jerusalem. But the principle of tithing was very clearly laid out to the church at Corinth: The offering was to be taken week by week and the offering was to be according to how they prospered. This is exactly what the Old Testament taught concerning tithing.

According to the foregoing principle man is plainly taught that God set tithing as a requirement on His people in both the Old and The New Testament. Therefore to withhold the tithe from God is stealing:

> Will a man rob God? Yet you have robbed Me. But you say, "In what way have we robbed You?" You have robbed Me in tithes and offerings. Because you and this whole nation have robbed me, you are cursed with a curse. Therefore bring all the tithes into the storehouse, that there may be meat in My house, and by doing so you may prove Me, say the Lord of hosts, and see if I will not open to you the windows of heaven, and pour out a blessing on you, that you will have more than you can store up (Malachi 3:8-10).

The sad part of stealing from God is that He has given all things to us. We would have nothing without Him. And what we withhold from Him, when we fail to tithe, is such a small part what He has given to us that we make ourselves small and totally selfish before a loving and generous God.

How ashamed and hurt He must be with such mean, hateful, stingy, and unloving children.

God wants to bless His children, but He cannot bless disobedience. Therefore, when we steal from God, we rob ourselves of the blessings of God.

## (Time For God)

We also need to understand that tithing includes more than money; it also includes our time. Surely God requires that we serve Him with our time. Scripture clearly teaches that we are to give Him some of our time every day of our lives. To not do so is to steal from Him just as surely as to not give Him our monetary tithe.

If a tenth of everything we possess belongs to God, and the Bible says that it does, then we owe Him at least sixteen hours and forty-eight minutes of each week as a tithe of our time. Before you say you give Him more than that, give some thought to how much time that really is. Attending the regular services of your church will add up to only five and one quarter hours per week, at the most, if your church is like mine. If you attend choir practice that will add, at the most, another hour and a half of your time to what you owe God. If you teach a Bible study class, add another three hours for study. You have now reached a grand total of nine hours and forty-five minutes. If you spend an hour each day in private devotions it will add seven more hours to the total. Now you have three minutes left over of the tithe of your time.

Let us look at those times again. There are really only two hours of that time that could be called time spent in service for God: The hour and a half spent in choir practice, and the three hours in preparing to teach. All the other time is really time spent in receiving blessings that God has for you. So, we find ourselves back to four and one half-hours spent in service for God.

Remember, it is time spent serving God, not time spent with God that is really part of the tithe of our time. Also remember, we have been dealing with a tithe of our time, and have made no mention of an offering of time made to God. You can withhold your offering of time and miss a blessing. If you withhold the tithe of your time, you are stealing time that belongs to God.

## (Talent For God)

Talents are given by God to be used for Him, whether it is the talent to play the piano, to preach or teach His Word, or whatever other useful ability He has given to you. Jesus gave us a clear warning in the story of the man who was given one talent:

> Then he who had received the one talent came and said, "Lord, I know you to be a hard man, reaping where you have not sown, and gathering where you have not scattered seed: And I was afraid, and went and hid your talent in the earth: see, here is what belong to you (Matthew 25:24-25).

There are too many "one talented" men in this world. They will not put themselves out in the least way for the Lord. Or, perhaps as the one-talented-man, they fear not being able to satisfy the Lord, so they do not do anything at all.

The answer of the man's master should make all such people pause and think:

> His lord answered and said to him, "You wicked and lazy servant, you knew that I reap where I did not sow, and gather where I have not scattered seed: You should have put my money with the banker, and then at my coming I would have received my own with interest. Therefore take the talent from him, and give it to him who has ten talents. For to every one that has shall more be given, and he shall have abundance, but from him who has not shall be taken away even that which he has. And take the unprofitable servant and cast him into outer darkness: there shall be weeping and grinding of teeth (Matthew 25:26-30).

He had stolen his master's right to benefit from the talent. How often do we steal the rights of our Lord and Master? He has a right to the use of our entire life.

## (Our Total Life)

Our whole life belongs to God. You rob God of this by rejecting Jesus. This is the most dangerous stealing of all. For to refuse to give God your life by receiving Christ Jesus as Savior is to take your life in your own hands. You reject the help of God in all things.

Included in your rejection is the refusal to allow God to prepare you for Heaven by the New Birth. The writer of the book of Hebrews says,

> Therefore we should pay careful attention to the things, which we have heard, lest at any time we should

let them slip. For if the word spoken by angels was true, and every transgression and disobedience received a just reward; How shall we escape, if we neglect the great salvation; which was first spoken by the Lord, and was confirmed to us by the Apostles; God also confirming the witness, both with signs and wonders, and with various miracles, and gifts of the Holy Spirit, according to His own will? (Hebrews 2:1-4).

You can reject Jesus, but you are stealing your life from God. The writer of Hebrews asks how we expect to escape the wages earned by our rejection of God's salvation. He says that everyone who did so before reaped what he or she sowed. In Chapter 10, verse 31, he says, *"It is* a fearful thing to fall into the hands of the living God." If you steal your life from Him, you will stand in the Judgment and answer to Him.

Paul had the answer to the whole question, when he said to the Ephesian Christians:

> Let him who has been guilty of stealing, not do it anymore: but rather let him use his hands to do honest work, so that he may have to give to those who are in need (Ephesians 4:28).

# Chapter 10
## A Witness For Christ Or Satan

(Exodus 20:16)
"You shall not bring false accusations against your neighbor."

### - Introduction -

This may be the most ignored Commandment of the Ten by men in the world today. The disregard of God's demand for truth is so prevalent that it can be seen in most of the streets and homes of our cities and towns.

I can remember a time when the old saying, "A man's word is his bond," was a basic practice in our world. However truth is now so little esteemed by man it appears he can voice a lie more easily than he can speak the truth. Listen to the conversations where there are two or more gathered together if you doubt the truth of this. Before you have listened to many such conversations it will become apparent how little regard there really is for obedience to this Commandment.

A man can worship idols, and we call him a heathen. When a man commits murder, his freedom or his life is taken. If a man is found guilty of adultery, we often condemn and shun him. But a man can play free and loose with the truth, and we accept him as our friend and companion. Is this not a sad commentary on our world that truth is of so little value?

God says the sin of lying is as evil as all other sins. It is evident that this is true, for He includes the prohibition of it in His Law: "You shall not bring false accusations against your neighbor." If He sets it among the other Laws then it stands on equal ground with the other Laws.

Since it is obedience that is demanded by God's Law, it is apparent that disobedience of one Commandment is as much sin as disobedience of another Commandment. Hold this thought; we will discuss it in Chapter 12.

To tell an untruth is to disobey God's Commandment therefore it is as wicked a sin as any other sin. With this thought in mind we need to observe that this Commandment speaks of:

### - The Witnessing Power Of Man -

The power of speech is one characteristic that sets man apart from animals. This is not to say that animals are unable to communicate with one another or with humans because it is evident they are able to do so. They have the ability to communicate their wants and feelings clearly. However, it is also evident that they do not have the ability to think rationally, nor convey rational thoughts. Man, however, has the power to intelligently convey thoughts and ideas through the medium of speech. Now it is true that some birds have the power to mimic speech, but it is a learned thing. They have no power to put thoughts together in intelligent speech. Only man has that gift of God, and what a wonderful gift it is. Surely we would not forget the source of this gift and thereby allow ourselves to use it unwisely or for evil purposes.

There are two miracles of exception to this limitation of animals to speak intelligently or rationally. Perhaps you will remember that one of these miracles of exception was performed on a donkey that belonged to a prophet named Balaam. God endowed the donkey with speech to convey a message of truth to His erring servant:

The people of Israel in their journey from Egypt came into the plains of Moab and camped across the Jordan River from Jericho. When Balak, the king of Moab, saw how many of them there were, and when he heard what they had done to the Amorites, he and his people were terrified.

Therefore, Balak sent a message to Balaam the prophet who was living in Pethor, near the Euphrates River. In the message he pleaded with Balaam to come and curse a people from Egypt who have invaded his borders. He told Balaam that he would then be able to drive them out of the land. He knew that those that Balaam blessed were bless greatly, and those that he cursed could not survive.

The messengers went to Balaam with money in hand and gave him Balak's message.

Balaam asked them to spend the night in his home. He would give them an answer in the morning as to what the Lord directed him to do. So they spent the night at Balaam's house.

That night God came to Balaam and asked him to explain the presence of the men from Moab and what they wanted.

He told the Lord that they were messengers from the King of Moab. And that a great host of people from Egypt had come to his border, and he wanted them cursed so that he would be able to drive them out of his territory.

God told Balaam that he was not to curse but bless those people.

When the morning came, Balaam told the men to go home because the Lord would not allow him to do what they wanted.

Balak's ambassadors returned and reported Balaam's refusal to come and curse Israel. Balak was not ready to give up on Balaam so he tried again. He sent more ambassadors to Balaam with another message.

The King promised greater honors plus any payment that he might ask: Balaam could name his own figure! All he had to do was come and curse the children of Israel for him.

However, Balaam replied that if the King were to give him a palace filled with silver and gold, he could do nothing contrary to the command of the Lord God. Balaam again invited the messengers to spend the night so that he could find out whether the Lord would add anything to what He said before.

That night God told Balaam that he could go with the men, but be sure to say only what He told him to tell them."

Very early the next morning he saddled his donkey and started off to Moab. But God was angry with Balaam because of his eager attitude, so He sent an Angel to stand in the roadway to kill him. As Balaam and two servants were riding along, Balaam's donkey suddenly saw the Angel of the Lord standing in the road with a drawn sword. She bolted off the road into a field, but Balaam hit her with his staff and drove her back onto the road. Then the Angel of the Lord stood at a place where the road went between two vineyard walls. When the donkey saw the Angel standing there, she squeezed past by scrapping against the wall, crushing Balaam's foot in the process. So he beat her again. Then the Angel of the Lord moved farther down the road and stood in a place so narrow that the donkey could not get by at all. So she lay down in the road. In a great fit of temper, Balaam hit her again with his staff.

Then the Lord caused the donkey to speak. First the donkey asked Balaam why he had beaten her. He told her it was because she had made him look like a fool. So Balaam told her that he wished he had a sword so he could kill her.

Then she asked him if she had ever done anything like this before in all her life. Balaam admitted that the donkey had never acted that way before.

Then the Lord opened Balaam's eyes and he saw the Angel standing in the roadway with a sword in his hand. The Word says that he fell flat on the ground before him. I suspect that he fainted.

There is no question that God got Balaam's attention by this miracle, but He did not get Balaam's obedience. The money and honor offered by Balak was too tempting to Balaam. Instead of taking God at His word the first time, he continued to want to go with the servants of Balak. The second time Balaam asked if he could go, God said he could. But this was only to teach Balaam a lesson. Is it not strange how man can experience the miraculous power of the Almighty and still desire to do the thing God said no to? Balaam's disobedience is a clear example of the destructive power of the sinful nature of man.

An even more familiar incident of a beast speaking is that of the serpent in the Garden of Eden. In this example, Satan was the one who conferred speech on it to convey a lie to Eve in Genesis 3:1-7.

In this situation Satan was successful in obtaining Eve's obedience. Is it not sad that we will listen to the lies of the Old Serpent in preference to the truth of God?

As astounding as these two exceptions to animals not being able to speak rational thought may be, it in no way changes the truth that man alone was created with this power to verbally communicate thoughts and ideas. Man alone was endowed with the power to be a witness in words.

## - Two Types Of Witness -

It is also abundantly clear that this Commandment speaks of two vastly different types of witness:

First, there is "the Witness of Truth." To this end, words are pictures of ideas and thoughts, and are intended to reveal the mind and the inward nature of the speaker. Since words show what is in the mind and nature of the person speaking, then it displays only what is there; it is a witness of truth. This is what John meant when he called Jesus "The Logos," which, simply put, means "the Divine Expression, the Word of God, the Truth, and the True Witness." John wanted the world to know that to Jesus was the essence of absolute truth. He was saying that Jesus was perfect and His words proved Him to be so. The words of Jesus revealed His perfect inward nature. Everything that Jesus said proclaimed that He was the perfect Son of God. He came to the world to show man the way of return God and to make God manifest to man. He was God in human flesh. Therefore the words of Jesus were the words of God. The words of Jesus opened the nature of God to be viewed by all who would look.

There are three words that illustrate "the witness of truth:"

The first word is "Simplicity," which means "singleness; the state or quality of being unmixed; the state of being not complex, or of consisting of few parts; artlessness of mind; freedom from subtlety or cunning; freedom from duplicity; sincerity" (Webster's New Twentieth Century Dictionary).

To obtain the full meaning of "simplicity" we must first run a reference on the word "simple." The dictionary says it means: "something not mixed or compounded; something having only one part, substance, etc"

(Webster's New Twentieth Century Dictionary).

It is evident "the witness of truth" is one who never has a double meaning in his words. He always avoids expressing complex or complicated thoughts, which might tend to confuse or obscure his meaning. You always know what he means. He never makes his words or ideas complicated, so there will be no misunderstandings. He says what he means and means what he says.

The second word is "Candor," which means "openness of heart; frankness; sincerity; honesty in expressing oneself. (Obsolete) Clearness; purity" (Webster's New Twentieth Century Dictionary). Openness, frankness, sincerity and honesty are excellent descriptions of the "witness of the truth." However I like one of the obsolete descriptions best of all, "Purity." That says it all. "The witness of the truth" will always be pure in words and deeds.

"Sincerity," is the third word, and it means "reality." But do we understand the meaning of "reality?" "Reality" is "The quality or state of being real" (Webster's New Twentieth Century Dictionary). "The witness of the truth" is never false. Nor is it a mere concept that has no basis in fact it is always real or genuine.

Then there is "the witness of evil."

Some politicians seem to say by their speech that words are intended to conceal ideas, and hide what is inside the speaker. If such is the basis for politics, then God deliver us from politics and politicians. Such would be evil in intent and in fact. Such witness is certainly contrary to God.

One title of Satan shows him to be the source of all evil witness: "The Devil," translated from the Greek, "diabolos." It means "slanderer, accuser, false witness and liar." No name has ever been more descriptive of it bearer than this title of Satan. Jesus confirmed this when He said to a group of Jews, who were intellectually in agreement with Him but not in heart agreement,

> Why do you not understand what I am saying? It is because you cannot hear My word. You are children of your father the devil, and you will do the evil of your father. He was a murderer from the beginning, and does not walk in the truth, because there is no truth in him. When he speaks a lie, he speaks of his own: for he is a liar, and the father of lies (John 8:43-44).

The sins committed by words are many. At the head of the list is Blasphemy, the impious or profane or vain use of God's name. This sin in word was covered in our discussion of the Third Commandment in Chapter four. It would be well to recall a part of that chapter: One common way that man can take God's name in vain is to use His name in jest, or to make Him the butt of a joke. Such irreverence causes His name to be held up to disrespectful laughter. Paul says that this ought not to be so: "Neither are obscene stories or foolish speech, nor crude jokes appropriate, but rather giving thanks to God" (Ephesians 5:4).

It is a dangerous thing to use God's name to swear falsely to something. This is called "stretching the truth" or "telling a white lie" or "playing loose with the truth" by those who do it. The truth of the matter is that it is plain and simple lying. That is exactly what Ananias and Sapphira did, and they died for it (Acts 5:1-10). This is true because it is profaning God's name: "And you shall not use my name to swear to a lie. For you to swear to a lie profanes, the name of your God: I am the Lord" (Leviticus 19:12). It is taking the name of God in vain.

The world is full of men who use God's name foolishly, through profanity or cursing. With some people, it seems, that every other word is a curse word or some kind of profanity. Instead of their speech being "always with grace, seasoned with salt" (Colossians 4:6) it is peppered with profanity and vulgarity. It chills my soul to hear the filth that pours from some peoples' mouth, men, women, and even children. It would appear that adults who talk with filthy language are lacking in vocabulary, to say the least.

When children, even four, five, and six years old, use vulgar language, it may be they have listened to adults talk this language of the gutter. Parents who set such an example will have much to answer when they face God.

Such people also fall into the same classification as those called "profane." Without question, they come under the same condemnation as those who are guilty of false swearing. The little epistle of James contains a stern admonition against this type of vain use of God's name: "Out of the same mouth comes blessing and cursing. My brothers and sisters, these things should not happen" (James 3:10). James is right; God's name should never be taken in vain. It should never be used irreverently.

Man needs to understand that God's name is holy. Over and over again we are told this in His Word: "You are to Glory in His holy name..." (Psalm 105: 3). "...holy and reverent is his name" (Psalm 111:9).

Mary, the mother of Christ, in her song of praise to God said, "For He that is mighty has done great things to me; and His name is holy" (Luke 1:49).

God's victorious children are pictured in the Revelation as saying, "Who shall not fear You, O Lord, and glorify Your name? For You alone are holy: for all nations shall come and worship before You; for Your judgments are made manifest" (Revelation 15:4). The Psalmist says, "The fear of the LORD *is* the beginning of wisdom: a good understanding have all they that do His commandments: His praise endures forever" (Psalm 111:10). It will be a certainty that if we fear the Lord we will "glorify" His name as holy.

The forgoing should clear up any misunderstanding about what blasphemy involves.

Perjury would stand next in line as the sin against legal truth, or the sin against the nation or corporate man. Instead of telling "the truth, the whole truth, and nothing but the truth," the perjurer will speak a lie to the court, judge, and jury. Such an individual puts our whole judicial system in jeopardy. He may cause an innocent person to be put in prison, or cause them to be put to death, if the death penalty is involved. He also may allow a guilty person to go free. The perjurer is a dangerous person to himself and to others.

If we would follow a descending order, then slander would be next in order. This is a destructive sin against an individual. Through false words the slanderer intends to destroy the character of his victim. He will use innuendoes, suggestions and direct lies to accomplish his evil deed. Satan used this method of attacking the credibility of God's word to Eve and Adam. First he said, "Has God said, 'You shall not eat of every tree of the garden?'" Here the intimation is that God may be questioned concerning His dealings with man. This lays the basis for the direct slander of God's character. Eve said that God had prohibited only one tree and that was because to eat of that tree meant death. Now Satan uses a direct lie to slander the truth of the Lord: "You will not surely die." Then he compounds the slander: "For God knows that in the day you eat from this tree, then your eyes will be opened, and you shall be as gods, knowing good and evil." By his slander he effectively snared Eve and Adam in the trap of unbelief.

Potiphar's wife effectively slandered Joseph's character and caused that innocent man to be put into prison (Genesis 39:10-20). It is true that "a woman scorned" can be terribly dangerous, but slander used by women or men is equally evil and destructive. It is a tool of the Satan himself.

Backbiting would follow close on slander's heels, with the main difference being that words spoken in backbiting could be true or false. Here the object is to do injury to the one being talked about. Proverbs 20:19, says it can simply be the revealing of secrets: "He that goes about as a gossip reveals secrets: therefore do not keep company with the man who speaks flattering words." First he will flatter you to win your confidence. Then when the confidence is revealed he will betray it by telling it behind your back. The warning is that we should avoid such people altogether: The King James Version say, "meddle not with him" A synonym for "meddle" is "peek," which means to "glance at," which tells us that we are not to even look at such persons; not even a "peek." Psalm 15:1-3, suggests a good reason for staying away from such people:

> Lord, who shall remain in Your house? Who shall dwell in Your holy hill? It is he who walks the way of honesty, and works righteousness, and speaks the truth in his heart. It is the person who does not speak words of slander, or who will not do evil deed to his neighbor, or take up a criticism against his neighbor.

Paul says the same thing about the slanderer; only he does it from the negative side:

> For God shows His anger from heaven against all the ungodly and unrighteous men who prevent the truth from being known...And because they did not like to keep God in their thoughts, He gave them over to a perverted mind, to do such things that are evil. Being filled with every kind of unrighteousness: sexual immorality, wickedness, greed, spitefulness; envy, murder, insolence, deceit, malice, gossips, slander, haters of God, despiteful, proud, boasters, inventors of ways to do evil things, disobedient to parents, without understanding, covenant breakers, without natural affection, cruel, unmerciful: Who knowing the judgment of God, that they which commit such things are worthy of death, not only do the same, but have pleasure in those who do so (Romans 1:18; 28-32).

Flattery, false suggestions, double meaning words, and exaggeration are all companions that stand in approximately the same relative position, of being used to convey more than is actually meant. Job, faced with the duplicity of his friends, understood how serious a crime is the use of flattery and its companions. His visitors called themselves friends to his face, but they would turn on him if they thought it was to their own profit. So he said of them, "He that flatters his friends for profit, let his children go blind" (Job 17:5). The Psalmist said that God also understood the evil of flattery. Israel would sin. God would punish. Israel would then mend their ways, but not for long: "Nevertheless they flattered Him with their mouth, and they lied to him with their words" (Psalm 78:36). How pious man can talk, until he thinks God is no longer paying attention, then like Israel he will change his whole song and dance.

Suppressive speech would fall next in line. How many times do we sin by failing to tell the whole truth? We simply withhold part or parts of the story so that we convey the idea we want the hearer to receive. This is what Abraham did when he visited in Gerar. He did not actually lie to Abimelech about Sarah's relationship to him, for she was his half sister (Genesis 20:12). However, he did not tell the whole story. He suppressed the part about her being his wife to protect himself. So in effect he lied because he did not tell the whole truth.

Regardless of how we may rank the forgoing sins in words they all still belong to the same family called "lying." They all have the same father: Satan. The Psalmist says this about such a witness, "What he speaks is smoother than butter, but there is war in his heart: his words were softer than oil, yet underneath they are drawn swords" (Psalm 55:19-21).

Such words may be as soft as a feather bed, but they will cut to the bone. They are like the razor honed and stropped to a keenness that will comfortably shave the heaviest beard from tender skin without making a nick. Such sharpness will also draw blood before pain is felt. Much blood is drawn by razor sharp words.

James in his little epistle has some exceedingly pertinent things to say about the tongue and man's misuse of it. Despite the fact it is a small part of the body, he makes it clear that the tongue possesses dreadful powers. He makes his point by saying it boasts of great things. In using the word "boast" we need to understand that he does not intend that this be seen as the use of unjust self-praise. This is clear when he describes how it sets fires that can burn out of control and cause terrible destruction.

He also calls it a "restless evil" that is continually causing trouble. The tongue is never satisfied with peace and quite. It must be constantly stirring up trouble. It is forever meddling in the affairs of others.

Then James adds that it is like a dangerous serpent full of deadly poison. It will strike at the most unexpected times. Its bite can cause most serious consequences.

When these powers are understood it becomes clear that the tongue's boast of being able to do great things is not an over-estimate (James 3:1-13).

God says the tongue must be kept under control: "You shall not bring false accusations against your neighbor" (Exodus 20:16).

The Psalmist had a deep and abiding understanding of the will of the Lord in this matter. Therefore he gave instructions to the young in knowledge and faith:

> Come, my children, and listen to me: I will teach you the fear of the Lord. Do you desires long life so that you may do good deeds? Then keep your tongue from evil words, and your lips from speaking lies (Psalm 34:11-13).

Do you see the importance of this? If one is to know the fullness of eternal life and that, which is good, then he must learn to control his tongue. Of course we know that Christ must accomplish this work in us through the work of the Holy Spirit. So we must be open to the Holy Spirit and allow Him to work in our life. We must, in the power of the Holy Spirit, learn to control our tongue. We must use the witnessing power of the tongue for the glory of God and not for evil purposes.

This Commandment is also a demand:

## - Man Is To Witness To The Truth -

First, look at the New Testament's interpretation of this overwhelming mandate. "Let your word be "yes, I will," or "no, I will not." For whatever you say that is more than this comes of evil" (Matthew 5:37). Be exceedingly careful of your words. Say what you mean and mean what you say. Otherwise your words become sin. Paul said that we must keep our words of witness pure:

> Let your conversation always be filled with grace, seasoned with salt, that you may know how you ought to answer every man (Colossians 4:6).
>
> Never allow unclean words to come out of your mouth, but only that which is good to the use for edification, that they may be ministers of grace to those who hear. And do not grieve the Holy Spirit of God, by which you are sealed until the day of redemption. Let all bitterness, wrath, anger, screaming, and evil words along with all malicious thoughts, be put away from you, (Ephesians 4:29-31).

In other words, season each word and sentence with the influence of our Lord's words:

> Anyone who teaches anything else, not consenting to wholesome words, even the words of our Lord Jesus Christ, and to the doctrine which is according to godliness; that person is proud, ignorant, and fond of arguments and words of strife. From such persons come envy, strife, railings, and evil ideas. They are perverse. They enjoy disputes and have corrupt minds. They are completely lacking truth. They think that gain is godliness. Whatever you do stay away from such persons (I Timothy 6:3-5).

We are also admonished to let all our words of witness be truth:

> This I say therefore, testifying in the Lord, that from this time forward you are not to walk as other Gentiles walk, in the vanity of their mind, having the understanding darkened, being alienated from the life of God through the ignorance that is in them, because of the blindness of their heart...But you have not learned this from Christ; if it is true that you have heard Him, and have been taught by Him, the truth is in Jesus: That you put off the former conversation of the old man which is corrupt and defiled by deceitful lusts; and be renewed in the spirit of your mind; And that you put on the new man, which is created by God in righteousness and true holiness. Therefore putting away lying, let every man speak truth with his neighbor: for we are members one of another (Ephesians 4:17-25).

It is so easy to open the mouth and let the words flow without regard to the consequences. My constant prayer has ever been, "Lord give me every word You want me to speak, and keep me from speaking one word more than I should." I suppose my memory of the Old Testament verbalization of this truth is what prompts me to make this prayer:

> Let the words of my mouth and the meditations of my heart be acceptable in Your sight, O Lord my God (Psalm 19:14).
>
> Keep watch over my mouth, O Lord; keep the door of my lips (Psalm 141:3).
>
> The mouth of the righteous is a fountain of life (Proverbs 10:11).
>
> A gentle tongue is a tree of life (Proverbs 15:4).
>
> Pleasant words are like a honeycomb, sweet to the soul, and health to the bones (Proverbs 16:24).
>
> A word fitly spoken is like apples of gold in settings of silver (Proverbs 25:11).

For whom do you witness Christian friends? Christ or Satan? If for Christ, then you will speak in truth. If for Satan, then your witness will be lies.

Who do you believe my lost friends?

Jesus said, "I am the way, the truth and the life: no man comes to the Father, except through Me" (John 14:6), and "For if you do not believe that I am the Christ, you will die in your sins" (John 8:24).

Satan says, "You will not surely die" (Genesis 3:4).Remember, Jesus is the True Witness and Satan is the father of lies.

# Chapter 11

## Inordinate Desires

(Luke 12:15-21)

(Exodus 20:17)
""You shall not covet your neighbor's household: his wife, his male or female servant, his ox, his donkey, or anything that belongs to your neighbor."

### - Introduction -

As the Ninth Commandment is the most ignored, the Tenth is, possibly, the most misunderstood. This is evident when we hear this Commandment quoted, "You shall not covet."

To understand this Commandment we must know the meaning of the word "covet." According to Webster's New Twentieth Century Dictionary it means, "to desire or wish for, with eagerness; to desire earnestly."

Paul tells us that we should: "Covet earnestly the best gifts: and yet I show you a more excellent way" (I Corinthians 12:31).

Since Paul would never encourage us to disobey God's Law there must be more to this Commandment than simply "you shall not covet."

What God is actually saying in this Commandment is, "You shall not covet...anything that is your neighbor's." The definitive words in the Commandment being, "anything that is your neighbor's." Therefore what is forbidden is not simply to covet or to desire something, but rather it is allowing desires to run wildly out of control. It is to desire something so much that you will do anything to satisfy your desire, even to harming or disfurnishing yourself, or someone else.

It is at this point that simple coveting or desiring becomes lust. This is precisely what the apostle Paul calls it:

> What shall we say then? Is the law sin? God forbid! Never! I would not have known sin is, except that I learned it from the law: for I would not have known lust, except the law had said, "You shall not covet (Romans 7:7).

Therefore, as used in this Commandment, "to covet" is to lust after something, or to have unrestrained, unbridled desire, or "Inordinate Desire." Such desire is sin, unless the thing desired will accomplish or help accomplish the perfect will of God.

"Inordinate Desire" is the sin that Salome, the mother of James and John, was guilty of in her request of the Lord:

> Then the mother of Zebedee's children came, and worshipped Him, with her sons, and desired something from Him. And He said to her, 'What do you want Me to do?' She said to Him, "Grant that my two sons may sit, the one on your right hand, and the other on the left, in your kingdom." But Jesus answered and said, "You do not know what you are asking. Are you able to drink of the cup that I shall drink of, and to be baptized with the baptism that I am baptized with?" They said to Him, "We are able." And He said to them, "You will surely drink of my cup, and be baptized with the My baptism: but to sit on my right hand, and on my left, is not mine to give, but it shall be given to them for whom it is prepared by my Father" (Matthew 20:20-23).

It is clear from the foregoing that Salome and her boys only wanted their selfish desires satisfied. They were certainly not seeking the advancement of the Kingdom of God.

It is also a mistake to say that this Commandment forbids the accumulation of property. It does neither the one, nor the other. If it did, it would run counter to the Eighth Commandment, "You shall not steal." To understand this we need to recall a part of what we studied in Chapter Nine:

Man has a right to space, and that right can be stolen from him. The prophet Isaiah raised this issue and pronounced a judgment on those guilty of this type of stealing.

> Woe to those who join house to house, and add field to field until no land remains, and they are left alone in the earth! (Isaiah 5:8).

Jezebel's theft of Naboth's vineyard (I Kings 21:2-16) is a clear example of an evil heart being the cause of stealing, and also an accurate illustration of stealing a man's rights of personal space.

Ahab saw that Naboth's land joined his, and that it was a choice piece of property. He approached Naboth with an offer to buy the land, but Naboth refused. It was his inheritance. He simply would not sell it for any price.

Ahab must have been a terribly spoiled individual. He must have never been told no, or refused anything. He went back to the palace, went to bed and refused to eat. When Jezebel found Ahab in this state she told him to rise and eat and be happy. She assured him that she would get the vineyard for him.

That wicked queen used her husband Ahab's power as king and gave orders to the elders of Naboth's city to hire evil men to give false testimony against Naboth so he could be put to death. So the deed was done, and Naboth was killed. When word arrived at the palace Jezebel told Ahab to go and take Naboth's vineyard.

God sent Elijah to meet Ahab in the vineyard and say to him:
> Because you have sold yourself to work evil in the sight of the Lord, consider that He will bring evil on you, and will destroy your descendants...And of Jezebel the Lord also said, 'The dogs will eat Jezebel's flesh by the wall of Jezreel (I Kings 21:20-21, 23).

God's Word makes it evident that Naboth had a right to retain his property, and Ahab had no right to steal that property. Within the framework of this truth is found man's right to acquire and keep property. If the Bible teaches this right, then it cannot be understood as prohibited by this Tenth Commandment. Therefore this Commandment speaks of:

## - The Evil Of Inordinate Desire -

The other nine Commandments prohibit the overt acts of sin. This Commandment deals with that which is at the very heart of sin. It prohibits the very desire to act out sin. "Inordinate Desire" is that uncontrolled desire that results in the overt acts of sin. In other words, if it were not for "Inordinate Desire," there would be no overt acts of sin in our world.

The writer of the epistle of James expresses the forgoing idea in this way:
> Let no man say when he is tempted, I am tempted of God: for God cannot be tempted with evil, neither does He tempt any man: But every man is tempted when he is drawn away of his own lust, and enticed. Then when Lust has conceived, it gives birth to sin (James 1:13-15).

The meaning is clear: "lust," or "Inordinate Desire," is the root and also the instrument of the root cause of every sin. Basically its name is "Selfishness." It is what the Bible calls "the Sinful Nature" or "the Nature to sin." This is the sin that separates man from God. The Apostle Paul verbalizes this idea as follows:
> And He has made you alive, who were dead in

trespasses and sins. That was the way you use to walk in time past according to the course of this world, according to the prince of the power of the air, the spirit who now works in the children of disobedience. Among whom we also all, in time past, had our way of life in the lusts of our flesh, fulfilling the desires of the flesh and of the mind; and were by nature the children of wrath (Ephesians 2:1-3).

Since "Inordinate Desire" is the evil prohibited here, it is evident that through the violation of this one Commandment man can and does violate all of the other nine Commandments. We can illustrate this fact by running this truth through each commandment.

Look again at the First Commandment: "You shall have no other gods before Me."

Job understood that "Inordinate Desire" is the root cause of man replacing God with other gods:

> If I have made gold my hope, and have said to the fine gold, you are my confidence; if I have rejoiced because my wealth was great, and because my hand had gotten much...this also would be an iniquity to be punished by the judges; for then I would have denied the God that is above (Job 31: 24-25, 28).

That which is most important to you is the god you serve. Therefore it is true what Job said. If you have an "Inordinate Desire" for riches, and put your trust in the power of riches, then it becomes your god because you have put it before the Lord God. You have violated the First Commandment, in that you are an idolater. Your "Inordinate Desire" or covetousness has made you a violator of the First Commandment as well as the Tenth Commandment.

Christ said it another way: "You cannot serve God and the things of this world" (Matthew 6:24; Luke 16:13).

Remember, the Second Commandment says, "You shall not make for yourself any carved image." We will let the Apostle Paul illustrate how this Commandment fits into violation of the tenth Commandment:

> For you know, that no sexually immoral, impure, or covetous man, who is an idolater, has any inheritance in the kingdom of Christ and of God...Therefore put to death your earthy ways; sexual immorality, impurity, lust, evil desires and greed, which is idolatry. It is for the sake of these things that the wrath of God falls on the children of disobedience (Ephesians 5:5; Colossians

3:5).

Paul makes it exceedingly evident in the above that covetousness is idolatry and a worshipping of images. Like the miser who pours out his gold; then looks at it lovingly, and runs his fingers through it as though caressing it. Therein we find the image of the god he worships and the violation of the Second and the Tenth Commandment.

The Third Commandment exhibits the same root cause: "You shall not speak the name of the LORD your God in a useless way." Or, "You shall not use God's name in witnessing to a lie."

That is exactly what Ananias and Sapphira did. They invoked God's name to witness that they paid over to the apostles all the money from the sell of their property (Acts 5:1-10). They had an "Inordinate Desire" to keep the money and to keep the respect of the others in the church, so they lied to satisfy those unholy desires. Therein they disobeyed both the Third and Tenth Commandments.

In the Fourth Commandment, "Remember the Sabbath day and keep it holy," we find the same cause of sin at work: "Inordinate Desire" for money:

> In those days I saw some men in Judah treading winepresses on the Sabbath, and bringing in bundle of wheat, wine, grapes, figs, and all manner of burdens and loading them on donkeys, which they brought to Jerusalem on the Sabbath day, and I testified against them...Then I challenge the nobles of Judah, and said to them "What is this evil thing you are doing: you are profaning the Sabbath day?" (Nehemiah 13:15, 17).

Then Nehemiah told what he did to stop this pursuit of profit on God's day:

> And it happened, that when darkness began to fall on the gates of Jerusalem before the Sabbath, I ordered that the gates be shut, and that they should not be opened until after the Sabbath: and I set some of my servants at the gates to see that no burden would be brought in on the Sabbath day. So the merchants and sellers of all kind of goods stayed outside Jerusalem once or twice. Then I asked them, "Why do you stay at the wall? If you do so again, I will lay hands on you." From that time forward they did not come back again on the Sabbath (Nehemiah 13:19-21).

Man's "Inordinate Desire" for monetary gain has always been an enticement for him to carry on secular work on the day that God said was meant to be a day of rest. This is true whether business is transacted on the Lord's Day, or if you mow your lawn. It is not that lawns are mowed on Sunday because there are no other hours available in which to do this work. It is done on Sunday because to do this job on business time would cost money. So this Commandment is disobeyed for the sake of an "Inordinate Desire" for money. Therefore, because of "Inordinate Desire," both the Forth and Tenth Commandments are violated.

This truth also applies to the Fifth Commandment: "Honor your father and your mother." How many instances can be recalled of "Inordinate Desires" being the cause behind a young man and woman despising the counsel or instruction of their mother and father? The instances are well documented, such as the two sons in the parable of the Prodigal (Luke 15:11-32), that it is unnecessary to mention further examples:

It is evident the father of those two boys loved his sons. I do not doubt that he counseled the younger son against taking his inheritance and leaving. However, this son's "Inordinate Desire" for freedom outweighed his desire to honor his father's words. We are told the father counseled the elder son to show love and compassion for his returning brother. There is no evidence the elder brother listened to his father's counsel. The overwhelming evidence is that he did not. His hatred for his brother and "Inordinate Desire" for revenge was stronger than his desire to honor his father's wishes. So they disobeyed the Fifth and the Tenth Commandments.

When we observe the reasons behind the widespread disobedience of the Sixth Commandment: "you shall not murder," they only confirm that "Inordinate Desire" is the root cause of all murder:

David had more than one reason for the murder of Uriah: His desire to possess Bathsheba was greater than his respect for the right of her husband to live. There was also his desire not to have his adulterous affair with Bathsheba found out, which was greater to him than the worth of Uriah's life. That is truly "unbridled lust" or "Inordinate Desire" in both instances. Therefore, without question, "Inordinate Desire" was the root cause behind the murder of Uriah, resulting in the violation of the Sixth and the Tenth Commandments.

Cain murdered his brother Abel in a jealous rage. His jealousy, however, stemmed from an "Inordinate Desire" to excel above his brother, and therefore it was also the root cause of the murder. Here we have a different "Inordinate Desire," but the result is the same as with David.

The Seventh Commandment, "You shall not commit adultery," is no different from the first six Commandments, in that "Inordinate Desire" is still the root cause. David and Bathsheba's story is again verification of this truth: David lusted after another man's wife. That is the "Inordinate Desire."

David's desire for Bathsheba was stronger than his desire for obedience to God's Law; therefore he took her and committed adultery. So he violated the Seventh and the Ten Commandments. There can be no question that "Inordinate Desire" was the root cause of David's sin.

An "Inordinate Desire" for money, or position, or for both has caused many a young woman to become a harlot. It was an "Inordinate Desire" for position that drove Tamar, the daughter-in-law of Judah to play the harlot with her father-in-law (Genesis 38:6-26):

When Judah's oldest son, Er, became a man, Judah arranged a marriage for him with a young woman named Tamar. Er, however, was evil in the sight of God, and so the Lord killed him.

Then Judah said to Er's brother, Onan, "You marry Tamar, so that she may bear children and heirs for your brother, as our law requires."

But Onan did not want to have a child who would not be his own. When he married her, and went in to have sex with her, he spilled the sperm on the bed so that she would not get pregnant. God did not approve of what Onan did so He killed him also.

Judah told Tamar not to marry again at that time. He said that she should return to her parent's home, and to remain a widow there until his youngest son, Shelah, was old enough to marry her. What he did not say to Tamar was that he really did not intend for Shelah to do this for fear that he would lose this son just as he had his two brothers. So Tamar went home to her parents, just as Judah requested.

Some time passed and Judah's wife died. When the time for mourning his wife was over, Judah and his friend Hirah went to Timnah to oversee the shearing of his sheep. Someone told Tamar that her father-in-law had left for Timnah, and realizing that she was not going to be allowed to marry Shelah, she laid aside her widow's clothing and covered her face with a veil so she would not be recognized. Then she went and sat beside the road outside the village of Enaim, which was on the road that Judah would have to travel to get to Timnah. When Judah passed by he saw her and thought she was a prostitute. So he stopped and asked her to have sex with him. He had no idea that she was his daughter-in-law.

He promised to send her a young goat as payment for her services. She wanted something to insure that he would send the goat so she asked him to leave something with her as a pledge. So he left his seal of identification and his walking stick. She let him have sex with her and, sure enough, she became pregnant. Afterwards she returned home and dressed again in her widow's clothing.

Judah sent his friend Hirah to take the young goat back to her and to get the pledges he had given her, but Hirah could not find her.

He asked the men of the city, if they could tell him where to find the prostitute who lived there. They told him they had never had a prostitute in their town. All he could do was return to Judah and tell him he could not find her, and what he had been told by the men of the town. They agreed that they could do nothing but let her keep the pledges.

About three months later someone told Judah that Tamar was pregnant. She had obviously played the harlot. Judah demanded that they burn her for her sin. But she sent a message to Judah along with his identification seal and walking stick and told him that the owner of these things was the father of her child.

Judah had no choice but to admitted that they were his and said, "She hath been more righteous than I; because that I gave her not to Shelah my son" (Genesis 38:26). And he never had sexual relations with her again.

Judah's statement that Tamar was more righteous than he is certainly no indication that either of them was righteous. He was simply admitting his failure to live up to his word with her concerning his son Shelah. Both were guilty of "Inordinate Desire" or they would not have found themselves in the dilemma they were in. An "Inordinate Desire" for sexual gratification that led to adultery or fornication, such as in the case of David with Bathsheba, and Judah with Tamar, can also lead to rape. It was this "Inordinate Desire" that led Shechem to rape Jacob's daughter Dinah:

> And Dinah the daughter of Leah, whom she bore to Jacob, went out to visit the daughters of the land. And when Shechem the son of Hamor the Hivite, prince of the country, saw her, he took her, and lay with her, and defiled her (Genesis 34:1- 2).

The violation of the Eighth Commandment, "You shall not steal," is obviously prompted by "Inordinate Desire." For it is surely an "Inordinate Desire" for money that motivates the mugger who waylays you to steal your wallet. That same "Inordinate Desire" also incites the burglar that enters your house by night and motivates the swindler who alters the company books, and prompts the con man to work his scam.

Now let us illustrate the violation of the Ninth and the Tenth Commandments together. To do this we will use Ahab's business dealings with Naboth that we looked at earlier on in the chapter.

Ahab looked and saw Naboth's vineyard and coveted it to the point that he could not accept the idea that he could not have it (violation of the Tenth Commandment). Naboth would not sell his vineyard, so Jezebel had two men bribed to swear to a lie (violation of the Ninth Commandment); put Naboth to death (violation of the Sixth Commandment); took his property (violation of the Eighth Commandment). It is evident that it was Ahab's covetousness, "lust," or "Inordinate Desire" that was the root cause of all these sins.

Now we see that this Commandment also speaks of:

## - The Destructiveness Of Inordinate Desires -

"Inordinate Desires" make a man poor toward God bringing him to total physical and spiritual bankruptcy. One of the best illustrations is our Master's story of the rich farmer:

>And one of the company said to Him, "Master, speak to my brother, and tell him to divide the inheritance with me." And He said to him, "Man, who made Me a judge or a divider of property over you?" And He said to them, "Take heed, and beware of covetousness: for a man's life does not consist in the abundance of the things which he possesses." And He told them a parable saying, "The ground of a certain rich man produced a great harvest. And he thought to himself, saying, 'What shall I do, because I have no room left to store my fruit?' And he said, 'I will do this: I will pull down my barns, and build larger ones; and I will store what I have harvested. And I will say to my soul, "Soul, you have much wealth stored up, and it will last for many years; take your ease, eat, drink, and be happy."' But God said to him, "You are a fool, this night your soul will be required of you: then who will get all these things which you have stored away?" So is everyone that stores up treasure for himself, and is not rich toward God (Luke 12:13-21).

Psalm 49 speaks succinctly to this truth:

>They trust in their wealth, and boast to themselves of how rich they are; yet they do not have the means to redeem their brother, or give God a ransom for him...so that he can live forever, and not die. For he sees that wise men die, likewise the fool and the degraded person perish, and leave their wealth to others. They think that their descendants shall continue forever, and their homes will stand for all generations to see; they name their lands after themselves. Nevertheless man...will not continue: he is like the animals that perish...Like sheep they are laid in the grave; death shall feed on them...and their

beauty shall be consumed in the grave...Therefore do not be afraid when one is made rich, when the glory of his house is increased; For when he dies he shall carry nothing away: his glory shall not follow after him (Psalm 49:6-16).

Alexander the Great obviously understood what the Psalmist had in mind. We are told he gave instruction that when he was buried his hands were to be left outside the bier, explaining that he wanted all to see they were empty. He, who had been king of the entire world, when dead, could keep none of it (*Encyclopedia Of 7,000 Illustrations*).

It is just as obvious that the Pharaohs of Egypt had absolutely no understanding of this truth. Their tombs were filled with gold, silver, and precious jewels; but there these precious things remained, keeping the embalmed bodies company, while the souls went to torment.

"Inordinate Desires" bring spiritual death. Remember what we read from James: "When lust has conceived, it brings forth sin..." He went on to say, "And sin, when it is finished, brings forth death." Paul says the same thing in Romans 6:23, "For the wages of sin is death..." Remember the Rich Farmer of our Scripture lesson. His soul was taken in spiritual and physical death. Remember the Rich Man, "And in hell he lifted up his eyes, being in torments..." Remember the Rich young Ruler:

> And a certain ruler asked him saying, "Good Master, what shall I do to inherit eternal life?" And Jesus said to him, "Why do you call me good? None are good, except one, that is, God. You know the commandments, 'Do not commit adultery, Do not kill, Do not steal, Do not bear false witness, Honor your father and your mother.'" And he said, "I have kept all these from my youth." Now when Jesus heard these things, He said to him, "You still lack one thing: sell all that you have, and give to the poor, and you will have treasure in heaven. Then come and follow Me." And when he heard this, he was very sad: for he was very rich. And when Jesus saw that he was very sad, He said, "How difficult it is for those who have riches to enter the kingdom of God!" (Luke 18:18-24).

If these things be true, and they are, then how much money may a man lawfully acquire under this Commandment? Can a rich man be saved? John wrote to Gaius, a rich man, "Beloved, I wish above all things that you may prosper and be in health, even as your soul prospers" (III John 2). If our soul will not grow spiritually while living in luxury, then we would be infinitely better off living in poverty. If we can take prosperity of soul with us, it is no sin to live in a palace. If ten thousand dollars will not lead our soul astray, then there is no harm in our having it. The same is true of a million or a billion dollars, if it does not interfere with the prosperity of our soul.

Jesus was perfectly precise in this matter:

> If any man will come after me, let him deny himself, and take up his cross, and follow me. For whoever will save his life shall lose it: and whoever will lose his life for my sake shall find it. For what is a man profited, if he shall gain the whole world, and lose his own soul? Or what shall a man give as payment for his soul? For the Son of man shall come in the glory of his Father with his angels; and then he shall reward every man according to his works (Matthew 16:24-27).

Now this Commandment speaks of:

## - The Way To Overcome Inordinate Desires -

Jesus gave the answer for conquering inordinate desires when he told Nicodemus that it starts with the new birth, "Truly, truly, I say to you, 'Unless a man is born again, he cannot see the kingdom of God" (John 3:3). This is the only way a man can rid himself of the "Inordinate Desires" that separate him from God.

The New Birth comes only through acceptance of the shed blood of Jesus Christ as your sacrifice for sin. Jesus said, "And as Moses Lifted up the serpent in the wilderness, even so must the Son of man be lifted up: That whoever believes on Him should not perish, but have eternal life" (John 3:14-15).

Without the New Birth we lose all hope of ever seeing God, and of ever being able to overcome Inordinate Desires.

# Chapter 12

## All, Or None At All

(James 2:10)
"For whoever obeys all the law but one is as guilty as if he had disobeyed all the Law."

### - Introduction -

With this chapter, we bring to a close our study of the Ten Commandments. I believe that what we will deal with here is as important, if not more important, than all the other eleven chapters, and it is a fitting end to our study. This chapter is the capstone of the study. Like the roof on a house, the house is incomplete without it, so this study is incomplete without this chapter.

In our text we find that:

### - The Commandments Are Equal In Importance -

Fellowship with God is the greatest blessing that man can know. Our daily walk with Him makes life worthwhile. Our communion with Him clears away the cobwebs of doubt and brings to us all of the insight and understanding we need to make the decisions we face every day. In that blessed fellowship with Him we find peace of mind that gives our heart and mind the joy to sing in freedom from fear. It is fear that destroys our peace. Fear must flee when light is present. For fear can only work its evil in darkness. Eternal light is found in the presence of and in fellowship with God. There is security when we walk hand in hand, in fellowship with God. Paul knew this well and expressed it clearly when he said,

> For I am persuaded, that neither death, nor life, nor angels, nor principalities, nor powers, nor things present, nor things to come, Nor height, nor depth, nor any other creature, shall be able to separate us from the love of God, which is in Christ Jesus our Lord (Romans 8:38-39).

David knew where his comfort and strength and peace were to be found:

> Even though I walk through the valley of the shadow of death, I will fear no evil: for You are with me; Your rod and Your staff protect me (Psalm 23:4).
>
> Truly my soul waits on God: from Him comes my salvation. He only is my rock and my salvation; He is my defense; I shall not be afraid of falling (Psalms 62:1-2).

Jesus wants us to rely on Him for nourishment and to know that our nourishment is found only in fellowship with the eternal triune God, so He said to us, "Think about the ravens: for they do not sow or reap; nor do they have storehouses and barns; and God feeds them: you are worth much more than the any birds?" (Luke 12:24).

Abraham accepted and followed this truth without question. When the Lord spoke to him, he heard and obeyed with an obedience that was born out of a close fellowship with the eternal God:

> Now the Lord had said to Abram, You are to leave your country, kindred, and your father's house, and go to a land that I will show you. And I will make you to become a great nation, and I will bless you, and make your name great; and you shall be a blessing. And I will bless them who bless you, and curse him that curses you. And through you all the families of the earth will be blessed. So Abram went, as the Lord had instructed him to go, and Lot went with him. Abram was seventy-five years old when he moved away from Haran. And Abram took Sarai his wife, and Lot his brother's son, and all their possessions and people that they had acquired in Haran; and they traveled toward the land of Canaan; and arrived in the land of Canaan (Genesis 12:1-5).

In Haran there was the stability of community and family. It is difficult to leave these without pain and distress. In fact, God was evidently sympathetic with this difficulty. He allowed Abraham to remain in Haran until his father Terah had passed on.

There was also the strength and security of the wealth that had been accumulated in Haran. Abraham had watched the flocks and herds become sleek with fat on the rich pasturelands of that well watered country between the rivers. He had counted the additions to his wealth and was staggered by how rich he had become in this fertile land. Such blessings are difficult to give up. However, fellowship with God was more important to Abraham. He could give up all that Haran represented for the blessed walk with God.

Abraham also displayed his faith in the worth of having, and the importance of maintaining fellowship with God when he went in complete obedience to Mount Moriah to offer his son Isaac as a sacrifice. Genesis 22:1-18 records the incident for us. There we find the fulfillment of Abraham's faith in the safety and comfort found in perfect fellowship with the living God.

These instances from the histories of Paul, Christ, David, and Abraham allow us to see just how important fellowship with God should be and is to His children. It is something that should never be taken lightly. We should cherish, guard, and protect our fellowship with Him with all that we have and are.

The Commandments are each equally important to our fellowship with God. To violate any one of the Ten Commandments is to sever that fellowship. God cannot fellowship with sin. Remember what happened to Christ on the Cross:

> Now from the sixth hour until the ninth hour darkness over covered the land. And about the ninth hour Jesus cried with a loud voice, saying, Eli, Eli, lama sabachthani? That is, My God, my God, why have You forsaken me? (Matthew 27:45-46).

The fellowship between the Father and His precious Son was broken because of the sins of the world that Jesus took upon Himself. If that was true of the sinless Son of God, who was infinitely and absolutely perfect, how much more will it be true of us in all our sinful imperfection?

The Ten Commandments are equally important to our service through the church. The violation of any one of the Commandments can damage that service. The violation of a Commandment is sin, and sin hardens the conscience, which tends to lead us further and further away from service. It also brings the charge of hypocrisy, which drives away those we are trying to win, thereby damaging our service through the church.

The Ten Commandments are equal in importance to our relationship with our fellowmen. When men keep the Laws of God there can be no strain in their relationship. They will live in harmony, one with the other. The violation of any one of the Commandments leads to a break down in the relationship of men. All of the wars that have been fought in this world, every incident of hate from man to man, every murder from the first to the last, every act of adultery, and every other evil that has beset society has come from disobedience to God's Law.

Now our text tells us that:

## - To Violate One Commandment Is To Violate All -

This is so because the Lawgiver is "One." Deuteronomy 6:4 says it, and Jesus verifies it in Mark 12:29, "Listen, O Israel: the Lord our God is one Lord." All Laws, therefore, possess the same Divine authority, just as it is recorded in Exodus 20:1, "God spoke all these words..." Since God is one and He spoke all these commandments into being, then to violate one Commandment is to violate the entire authority that ordained the whole Law. Therefore the guilt for disobedience of one Commandment is the same as the guilt for disobedience of all the Commandments. When you violate one of God's Commandments you are saying to Him I reject Your Authority to make these Laws.

It follows from this that the Law itself is one. Jesus summed up the Ten Commandments this way:

> Jesus said to him, "You shall love the Lord your God with all your heart, and with all your soul, and with all your mind." This is the first and father of all commandments. And the second is similar to it; "You shall love your neighbor as yourself." All the law and the prophets sprang from these two commandments (Matthew 22:37-40).

Therefore the Law is one in love for God and man. Disobedience of one law then hurts the heart of God as much as if all were disobeyed. Also, love for God does not allow for the disobedience of one or all of God's Commandments without paying the same penalty of broken love whether it be for disobedience to one or all of the Commandments. Love for God will rise up in the mind and heart and the pain that the disobedience brings will be as severe on that one who is guilty of disobedience to one of God's Laws as if he was guilty of disobedience to all the Law.

Perhaps the following similes will help to enforce the comparison in our minds: The Law is like a seamless robe. It is torn when only part is torn; The Law is like musical harmony. It is marred if one voice is singing out of tune; The Law is like a necklace of Pearls. A single pearl cannot be dropped without breaking the string upon which the others hang, so that all fall to the ground.

It follows from this that the spirit of obedience to the Law is one. True reverence for the law is inspired by love for the Lawgiver. Therefore obedience is impartial. Obedience strives to be perfect. Love for the Lawgiver will see each of the Laws as equal. The man who violates one of the Commandments shows that, in principle, he is disloyal to the Lawgiver. Therefore he would violate any of the other Commandments were he exposed to similar temptation to do so. This bears out our text, "Offend in one point...guilty of all."

Yes, the Commandments are of equal importance; therefore let, us contemplate our obligation to render perfect obedience to the whole Law of God not just the ones that suit our fancy.

We must consider, however, that it is impossible to render perfect obedience to the whole Law in and of ourselves. The nature of man is to sin. Therefore we need to understand the necessity of being clothed with the righteousness of Christ.

Every individual stands guilty of violating all of God's Law. But there is a difference in the way these appear to God. The one who has accepted Christ, as Lord and Master, stands before God clean and pure not because they are less sinful, but because through Jesus Christ their sins are forgiven. The one without Christ stands before God guilty and condemned. not because they are more sinful, but because they have no sacrifice or covering for sin. How do you appear to God?

## - The End -